Super Simple

MEDITERRANEAN DIET COOKBOOK FOR SENIORS

Eat Healthy, Support Longevity & Control Weight
— Your Complete Science-Backed Guide with Easy,
Delicious Recipes Anyone Can Make!

HANNAH LAUREN COSTA

Table of Contents

Introduction

Why This Book?

The older we get, the more conscientious we are about our daily habits that affect our health. It's much easier to be aware of the routines that affect our health because of the drop in energy levels and more frequent aches, as well as longer discussions with the doctor about blood pressure and cholesterol. While we can't turn back time, we can change the way we eat.

The Mediterranean diet is the perfect way of adjusting your diet without feeling like you are sacrificing the foods you love. It encourages people to eat slower, socialize while they eat, and focus on consuming fresher foods that are more nutritious.

With so many fad diets and books full of complicated meal plans available, it's understandable that you are skeptical of any diet book. What differentiates this book from the others is that it focuses on the basics and concepts that you already know. You don't need your own chef or a fridge full of expensive foods to eat well and feel better.

You need a simple solution that you can follow without having to constantly think about it. You need a plan that adapts to your life, not you adapting to the diet. This is what makes for a sustainable diet that changes your habits, not a short-term solution to meet a short-term goal.

That's exactly what this book offers – a simple solution that feels like you are improving your life, not just your health.

What's really great is that the Mediterranean diet isn't restrictive. Instead, it encourages you to be mindful as you eat and choose non-processed foods most of the time. No food is forbidden. This makes it easier to feel good about choosing better foods – there is no guilt when you eat a meal that isn't quite as healthy as usual.

This book provides you with the information you need to eat well, be healthier, and live better.

Why the Mediterranean Diet?

One of the things that makes the Mediterranean diet stand out from other diets is that it isn't a fad or short-term solution. It offers a way of slowly adjusting how you eat so that you learn to eat healthier without there being a huge interruption to your life. What it teaches you is how to eat like the people who live longer than almost anyone else in the world – Greece, Italy, and Spain. Their diet is a large reason why they live longer and with fewer health problems.

The diet focuses on foods that are more nutritious and natural.

- Lots of vegetables and fruits
- Olive oil as the main fat
- Beans, lentils, and whole grains
- Nuts and seeds
- Fish and seafood
- Occasional dairy and poultry
- Very little red meat or processed food

The diet is also very flexible. Notice that on the list no food is banned. You can still eat those foods, but you focus on the healthier foods to make up most of your diet. You should not only enjoy the food but the process of preparing your meals.

By making the changes, you'll start to see a positive effect on your body and overall health. You'll learn how to make delicious foods that you can enjoy without feeling like you are missing out. You'll especially notice it as you begin to feel better, with fewer aches and more energy.

..d it isn't just in the minds of people who make the change. There is scientific evidence that supports the positive effects the diet has by those who follow it:

- Reduces the risk of heart disease and stroke
- Lowers blood pressure and cholesterol
- Improves blood sugar control
- Helps with weight management
- Supports brain health and memory
- Reduces inflammation

Unlike so many other diets, the Mediterranean diet leaves you feeling full and satisfied with your meals. It enhances your life instead of making you feel like you are being punished.

The ingredients are both healthier and accessible. You don't need to hunt down expensive foods to eat well; you just need to be more discerning in what you buy. Nearly everything in this book is available at your local supermarket, and the best foods are probably at your local farmer's market.

Why It's Great for Seniors

We should be taking care of our bodies from an early age. And while you can't undo the unhealthy habits you had in your youth, as you reach your golden years, you can be more careful of what you eat to improve your health and energy levels going forward. The Mediterranean diet gives you a natural way to get all of the nutrients you need from your meals:

- **Healthy fats** for brain health and joint flexibility
- **Fiber** for digestion and blood sugar control
- **Antioxidants** that fight cell damage and support immunity
- **Calcium** and **magnesium** for strong bones
- **Protein** from fish, legumes, and dairy for muscle health

Numerous studies have shown that the Mediterranean diet helps reduce many health risks, such as the following:

- Heart disease
- High cholesterol
- Type 2 diabetes
- High blood pressure
- Arthritis
- Memory loss
- Osteoporosis

The meal isn't just about eating nutritious food though. It's about a healthier lifestyle where you slow down and focus on the moment as you enjoy cooking and eating healthier, delicious foods. It helps provide a physical and emotional balance that makes life better.

The diet promotes:

- Better energy
- Improved mood
- Less digestive discomfort
- A stronger sense of routine and purpose

What people like the most about the diet is that it is a plan that most people can easily follow, especially as they get accustomed to the dietary changes. You start small, making little changes and substitutes to your current diet until you don't even realize that you've adapted to a healthier diet and don't even miss the foods that you used to eat all of the time.

What is the Mediterranean Diet?

A Simple Explanation

The Mediterranean diet is an actual diet - it isn't a fad or quick solution. It doesn't tell you what to eat or not eat, how many calories you are consuming, or track your meals. It's about changing what you eat to a more traditional diet that has helped people in and around the Mediterranean Sea to live longer, healthier lives. This is why the diet is more likely to not only work to help you lose or maintain a healthier weight, but it is a diet you can sustain over the rest of your life.

For generations, people in the Mediterranean have eaten natural, healthy foods regularly. They don't have to think about it because it is just a part of their usual day. They are accustomed to reaching for fresh vegetables, fruits, and legumes for snacks, and their meals frequently include olive oil, fish, and herbs. Meats aren't the primary component of the meal. Instead, they are just one component of a repast that is rich in vegetables, whole grains, and other nutritious foods.

Another important part of this way of life is enjoying meals with others. People sit down to eat and talk. As people socialize, they eat more slowly, giving them more time to register that they are full. As a result, they are far less likely to overeat.

This is why it is much more likely to lead to better results – it is a way of life that is easy to adapt to a part of daily living. It's simple and enjoyable, and over time, you'll notice that it works.

This book provides tips and tricks that help you gradually adjust your diet to align with the Mediterranean diet. You won't need to memorize a bunch of numbers for the calories you eat or learn some new food pyramid. Instead, this book focuses on what actually matters when it comes to diet: making healthy choices in a way that feels natural, not like an obligation.

Origins and Core Principles

The diet has been around for centuries, but the model in this book is based on eating habits and traditions in the Mediterranean area during the 1950s and 1960s. That's around the time that people, particularly researchers, noticed that the people who lived in places like southern Italy and rural Greece were living longer and had lower rates of heart disease and other chronic ailments, even though these areas were not as well off as other parts of Europe. Residents weren't wealthy and they didn't make concentrated efforts to exercise more. They seemed healthy without relying on fad diets, tools, or equipment.

Curious to know the reason why, researchers started paying attention to local residents' daily and seasonal habits. Residents ate home-cooked meals with fresh, local foods. They ate the foods that were available at that time, so their diets changed based on the time of year. They got different foods based on what plants were in season. They ate food from nearby orchards and farms, fish from the Mediterranean, and olives pressed from nearby groves. Since there weren't many cattle, red meat made up only a small part of their regular diet, and it was often more like a garnish than a main course. Their proteins were primarily plant-based or from fish. Dairy was often included in their meals in small amounts, usually yogurt or cheese, giving them an additional source of protein.

However, there were other differences that went beyond just nutrition. People in the region had a more relaxed way of living. They didn't rush through meals; instead, they savored their food and chatted as they ate with family and friends.

They spent a lot of time walking, not to lose weight, but instead of using cars or other motorized vehicles. They rarely snacked, and when they did eat, food was treated as more than just fuel for the body. It was an enjoyable experience that enhanced their lives.

Over time, researchers realized that the people who inspired the Mediterranean diet didn't follow fads or marketing schemes. They weren't swayed by commercials and radio ads. They did what they had always done, and it proved to be far more effective and healthy. They had a lower risk of heart disease, strokes, diabetes, and Alzheimer's. They were also less likely to get some types of cancers.

There are many variations of this diet because the regions of the Mediterranean that follow the diet are varied with a lot of different foods. For example, people living in Spain are more likely to eat a lot of fish than those who live in Italy and Greece. Italians consume more pasta, and Greeks are more likely to have yogurt as a regular part of their diet. However, there are a few core principles:

- Eat mostly plant-based foods: vegetables, fruits, beans, lentils, whole grains
- Use healthy fats, especially olive oil
- Eat fish and seafood regularly (about 2-3 times a week)
- Enjoy dairy in moderation (mainly yogurt and cheese)
- Limit red meat, processed foods, and added sugars
- Stay physically active and socially connected
- Eat slower and savor meals

These are just general guidelines though, not hard and fast rules. This way of living is incredibly flexible, and it should be personalized to meet what's locally available in the area where you live.

As a senior, flexibility is incredibly important because your body is already changing and you have to be more aware of those changes. Your appetite isn't the same as it was in your 20s or even your 50s. Your ability to do vigorous exercises isn't what it used to be. If you live alone, you may not be as motivated to do a lot of cooking. Or if you're retired, you might enjoy having more time to cook for friends and loved ones. Whatever approach you want to take is perfectly fine, as long as you are moving toward eating more naturally and simply. You should be choosing these kinds of foods over highly processed foods that are full of empty calories and sugar. You don't need to follow every aspect of the diet to experience its benefits. Adopting a few core habits is enough to see some big improvements in the way you feel on a daily basis.

It's Not About Restriction – It's About Balance

The Mediterranean diet focuses on what you should eat without telling you what you *can't* eat. The focus is on adding good foods, more fiber, healthy fats, and a lot more color from plants. Meals become something to enjoy, not something to dread.

This is a welcome change for a lot of people, especially as we age. We are already told new rules and ways we need to be restrictive in our eating to be healthy. It's easy to develop anxiety and guilt around eating, which just makes it more likely that we won't eat well.

The balanced and more mindful approach of the Mediterranean diet is easier to follow without feeling like we are doing something wrong. It encourages connecting with others and enjoying your food. You can have a glass of wine with your dinners (this is very common in the Mediterranean region), and you can enjoy a nice slice of cake for your birthday or upcoming celebration. You can enjoy all of these guilt-free because you aren't cheating on a strict diet; you're maintaining a healthy diet while still enjoying some of your favorite foods.

Here are some of the things that you can enjoy to establish a balanced diet:

1. **Have oatmeal with fruit in the morning**, but don't feel bad if you occasionally enjoy a slice of toast with a little jam.
2. **Replace butter with olive oil and be generous with it** for cooking and dressings, but skip deep-fried foods that leave you feeling heavy.
3. **Enjoy a piece of fish two or three times a week**, but if you miss a day, it's not a problem.
4. **Snack on nuts or fruit** instead of chips or candy, but know that one treat won't ruin your progress.

If you are dealing with less appetite or energy, this approach will be so much easier than overhauling your diet. You'll learn how to choose healthier foods over time, as well as appreciate how it changes the way you feel. The diet is also surprisingly satisfying, so you aren't likely to want to eat nearly as often.

The following are some of the main ways seniors have reported feeling better after starting to adjust to the Mediterranean diet.

- Regain enjoyment in food
- Reduce reliance on medications
- Improve digestion and regularity
- Sleep better and wake up with more energy
- Feel a greater sense of control over their health

It's also nice to actually take time to eat and enjoy your meal. Sitting down and focusing on the food and chatting is just a nice way to keep your mind in the present and enjoy the day. It helps you to eat slower so that you will eat less and feel fuller longer. This also helps you to better digest your food.

In Summary

Since this isn't a diet that requires a strict approach, you won't feel resentful or guilty just for eating something you want to enjoy. You can broaden your palate while boosting energy and improving your health. Best of all, the foods are incredibly tasty and visually appealing.

We'll take a closer look now at how seniors benefit from this diet, what foods to focus on, and how to cook a much healthier and balanced diet.

Remember, this is about feeling more energetic and stronger, not trying to feel younger. The fact that you get to enjoy what you eat makes the whole experience that much better.

Health Benefits for Seniors

You don't want to just live longer; you want to live better. You want to feel good when you are getting out of bed and going about your day. While some physical and cognitive decline is inevitable, you can minimize it with the right diet.

Scientific evidence shows that the Mediterranean diet is incredibly effective in helping people live longer, better lives. While it doesn't entirely prevent disease, it can significantly reduce so many risks and discomfort that come with aging. Because so many of the foods are anti-inflammatories, people who follow it have stronger joints, more energy, and think more clearly.

Heart Health

Heart health is something that we all know is important, but we tend to neglect it until we start to have problems. That's one of the reasons why heart disease is the leading cause of death around the world, especially for people over 60 years old.

The Mediterranean diet helps to reduce stress on the heart because so many of the foods that are important parts of the diet are very heart healthy. These foods help lower bad cholesterol while raising good cholesterol. It also lowers blood pressure, helps manage weight, and supports healthy circulation.

Here are the foods that are the biggest contributors to what makes this diet so heart-healthy:

- **Olive oil** is the main fat in this diet, and it is rich in monounsaturated fats, which are great for your arteries.
- **Nuts and seeds** provide healthy fats and plant-based compounds that improve cholesterol levels.

- **Fish** (like salmon, sardines, and mackerel) are packed with omega-3s—fatty acids that reduce inflammation and help prevent clots.
- **Whole grains, beans, fruits, and vegetables** are full of fiber, which helps keep your arteries clean and your blood sugar steady.

Research into the effects of the Mediterranean diet for seniors showed that they were at 30% lower risk of heart attack, stroke, and heart-related deaths compared to those with a more typical low-fat diet.

Brain Function & Memory

One of the most frustrating things about aging is that our minds simply aren't what they used to be. Our memories aren't quite as good as they once were, and it takes longer to reach conclusions. Ailments like dementia and Alzheimer's are becoming more common for older people.

The Mediterranean diet can help keep your mind much sharper because the foods help keep the brain healthier. The symptoms and problems of diseases like dementia can even be reduced (although not entirely prevented). In some cases, the Mediterranean diet actually helped improve cognitive health.

Here are the reasons why this diet is so beneficial to the brain:

- Many of the foods are anti-inflammatory, which helps reduce the damage to brain cells over time.
- Many of the foods are rich in antioxidants (found in berries, leafy greens, olive oil, and herbs), which protect against cognitive decline.
- The diet includes a steady supply of omega-3 fatty acids from fish and nuts, which are crucial for brain function and mood.
- Whole grains and legumes provide steady energy to the brain by keeping blood sugar levels stable.

Studies have shown that seniors who follow the Mediterranean diet score better on memory tests and are less likely to develop dementia. They also have slower rates of brain shrinkage. They can focus better, think more clearly, and even experience improved mood.

Joint Health & Anti-Inflammation

We expect to experience achy joints, knees, hips, and nearly everything else when we get older. The expectation is very different from the experience. Minor aches and pains should be expected, but diet plays a large role in how much pain you are likely to experience. Highly processed foods increase inflammation, which contributes to these pains, especially arthritis pain.

The Mediterranean diet actually reduces inflammation, which means that your body hurts less. That's because a lot of natural foods are anti-inflammatory. Seniors who follow it are more likely to see improved mobility, reduced swelling, and less joint pain.

Here are the most common foods in the diet that are anti-inflammatory:

- **Olive oil**, especially extra virgin
- **Fatty fish**, like salmon and sardines
- **Leafy greens**, such as spinach and arugula
- **Berries and colorful fruits**, which are high in antioxidants
- **Legumes**, like lentils and beans

Processed and fried foods both make inflammation worse, as do foods with added sugars. One study showed that seniors who adopted the Mediterranean diet started experiencing reduced joint pain and stiffness after 12 weeks on the diet. Participants were able to sleep better, move around more easily, and required pain medications less frequently.

Even if you don't eliminate pain, you will feel a lot better. The small improvements you'll start to notice early on when you are following the diet can motivate you to keep eating healthier.

Longevity & Energy

Besides the physical and mental health benefits, the right diet gives you more energy and helps extend your life. The Mediterranean diet is associated with longevity and a higher quality of life. In some places, particularly in Sardinia and the surrounding area, people regularly live into their 90s with minimal illness. These areas are called the Blue Zones to indicate the high quality of life and longevity.

The following are the ways this diet contributes to helping you stay strong and active well into your senior years.

- The diet provides consistent, steady energy.
- The diet supports muscle strength with healthy protein from fish, legumes, and dairy.
- It helps prevent fatigue caused by blood sugar crashes or processed food overload.
- The diet reduces the risk of chronic diseases that often limit independence.

With the Mediterranean diet, food isn't just a source of fuel; it's something enjoyable that can extend your life. It gives you a reason to cook, share, and stay connected to the people around you. Besides health benefits, it has a lot of social benefits that enhance each meal.

People who follow it also find that they have more stamina. They feel less sluggish and bloated because they eat more slowly and notice when they are full before overeating.

The fact that the Mediterranean diet improves quality of life, not just longevity, is the reason why it has become so popular. And why it will likely remain a preferred diet to improve nearly every aspect of a person's life, especially when they reach their senior years.

Core Foods Made Simple

Changing something as fundamental as your diet isn't easy. Trying to make the change all at once makes it far more likely that you will fail. A lot of diets also expect you to memorize rules and calculations to succeed. That's why people tend to fail when they try new diets.

This chapter provides the details about how to make the change in a way that will be easier to follow. You'll learn what foods are preferred, what foods to minimize in your diet, and which foods are fine in moderation. The goal is to be smart about your choices.

What to Eat More Of

At its foundation, The Mediterranean diet is about eating real, unprocessed foods that you can get locally. The food is fresh, so it doesn't come in packages. The ingredients are easily recognizable because they are fresh. These are the foods that fill you up for longer and give your body a much more consistent energy source.

Let's look at the foods that can improve your life as you alter your diet.

Fruits and Vegetables

We all know that we should be eating a lot of fruits and vegetables, but people around the Mediterranean show exactly what the benefits are. They are proof that eating plenty of fruits and vegetables works.

Here are the things that fruits and vegetables provide that make them such an important part of healthier eating:

- **Fiber** to keep digestion smooth and steady
- **Antioxidants** to protect your cells and help prevent disease
- **Vitamins and minerals** that your body needs, especially as you age

Here are some general guidelines about them:

- Eat at least 2 servings of fruit per day (fresh, frozen, or unsweetened dried)
- Eat at least 3 servings of vegetables per day, especially leafy greens, tomatoes, peppers, zucchini, onions, eggplant, and carrots

Things to make them more enjoyable:

- Cook veggies until tender if chewing is a concern
- Make soups, stews, or purees if raw veggies are hard to digest.
- Cook frozen vegetables if it is easier—they're just as nutritious and last longer

These should be among the most important parts of your meals, but that doesn't mean getting accustomed to eating salads every day. It means adding a lot more color to your plate; fruits and vegetables are incredibly visually appealing because they come in bright oranges, deep greens, reds, and purples. The more color produce has, the more nutritious it is.

Olive Oil

This is where the real difference is – extra virgin olive oil is a main component of the Mediterranean diet. It has a lot of healthy fats, and it is very heart-healthy. They often use it instead of butter as a way of adding more flavor to the food.

Here are the ways that olive oil helps the body:

- Supports heart health
- Helps reduce inflammation
- Aids in nutrient absorption (especially vitamins A, D, E, and K)

And here are all of the ways you can use it:

- Cooking vegetables or fish
- Dressing salads
- Dipping bread (instead of butter)
- Roasting or baking

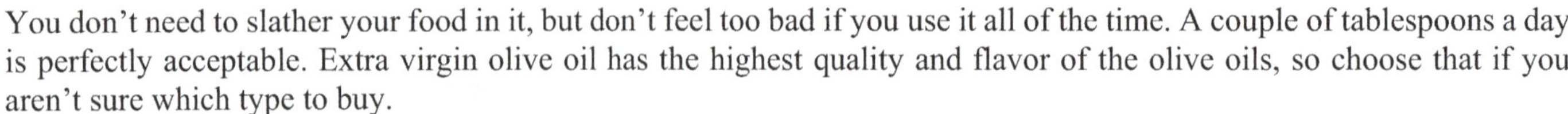

You don't need to slather your food in it, but don't feel too bad if you use it all of the time. A couple of tablespoons a day is perfectly acceptable. Extra virgin olive oil has the highest quality and flavor of the olive oils, so choose that if you aren't sure which type to buy.

It may take a little while to get used to it, especially if you are accustomed to using butter. That's why you should slowly add it, changing a meal or two every week to include olive oil instead of butter or margarine. Once you get used to it, you'll find it's very easy to add it to your daily diet.

Fish and Seafood

Fish is easily the most commonly consumed meat in this diet (although not necessarily the biggest source of protein). It's light, so you won't feel over full, and your body will be able to digest it much more easily than other types of meat. The best thing about fish though is how nutritious it is. Fatty fish are rich in omega-3 fatty acids, which are good for the brain, heart, and joints.

Here are the healthiest fish options:

- Salmon
- Sardines
- Mackerel
- Herring
- Trout
- Anchovies

Generally, plan to have fish for two or three meals every week. They can be fresh, frozen, or even canned. Really, the only fish you should minimize is breaded and fried – those have been cooked in a way that makes them far less healthy.

If fish isn't something you really enjoy, here are a few ways you may find it more palatable:

- Tuna packed in olive oil
- Fish soups or stews with herbs and tomato
- Mixing small bits of fish into rice, pasta, or veggie dishes

You don't need to have a large piece of fish – mixing it into foods with a lot of flavor will give you the nutrition you need without all that fishy taste.

White Meat (Poultry, Turkey, Rabbit)

The other primary types of white meat are fine in moderation, especially chicken and turkey.

Here are the reasons why they are preferred:

- Poultry is leaner than red meat.
- It is easier to digest.
- This meat is a good source of protein without a lot of fat.
- Poultry is versatile and familiar to most people.

If you have it a couple of times a week, that is just fine, especially as your source of protein between eating meals containing fish. Plant-based foods are the primary focus, and fish are secondary. Other types of meat are great for mixing things up, but they aren't as healthy.

Here are some of the ways people around the Mediterranean prepare poultry to get the best results.

1. Choose skinless cuts to reduce saturated fat
2. Bake, grill, or stew instead of frying
3. Use herbs, lemon, garlic, and olive oil for flavor
4. Combine with vegetables, grains, or legumes to create balanced meals

Here are a few examples of ways you can add white meats to your meals:

- Grilled chicken with roasted peppers and whole-grain couscous
- Turkey meatballs with tomato sauce and lentils
- Rabbit stew with white beans and herbs

Here are the types of chicken and cooking methods you should minimize:

- Processed or breaded chicken products
- Deli meats like turkey slices with added preservatives
- Over-relying on poultry at the expense of fish or legumes

White meat is great for seniors, especially if you are accustomed to red meat, but it should be a small part of a rotation of protein sources. Only on rare occasions should it be the main course.

Legumes (Beans, Lentils, Chickpeas)

This plant-based source of protein is incredibly powerful, especially if you are in your golden years. Legumes are high in fiber and protein, which makes them incredibly filling.

Here are the major benefits of legumes:

- They improve blood sugar control.
- They help manage cholesterol.
- They are great in supporting digestive health.

Here are the best types of legumes:

1. Lentils (red, green, brown)
2. Chickpeas (great for hummus or soups)
3. White beans, black beans, kidney beans
4. Fava beans, split peas

Here are a few ways to really enjoy them:

- Use canned beans for convenience (just rinse them well)
- Add to soups, salads, or stews
- Make bean spreads or dips for snacks

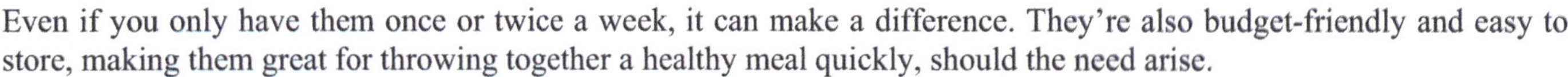

Even if you only have them once or twice a week, it can make a difference. They're also budget-friendly and easy to store, making them great for throwing together a healthy meal quickly, should the need arise.

Whole Grains

Whole grains are a fantastic source of energy, fiber, and nutrients without causing high blood sugar spikes.

Here are some of the most popular types of whole grains:

- Whole grain bread (look for 100% whole wheat)
- Brown rice
- Barley
- Farro
- Oats
- Whole grain pasta

Here are the ways whole grains help your body:

1. Improve digestion
2. Keep you fuller longer
3. Lower your risk of heart disease and type 2 diabetes

You shouldn't try to make this change all at once. Just start swapping refined grains with whole grains a bit at a time. Your body will take time to get accustomed to different grains. The slow introduction of whole grains will make that process go more smoothly. You'll find the change is well worth the effort.

Nuts and Seeds

These are foods that you probably already love and enjoy, so hearing that they are an important part of the Mediterranean diet is probably very welcome. You aren't likely to need to change too much.

Nuts and seeds pack a lot of nutrition in very small packages. They have a lot of healthy fats, protein, and essential minerals.

Here are some of the best nuts and seeds in terms of nutrition:

- Almonds
- Walnuts

- Pistachios
- Sunflower seeds
- Chia seeds
- Flaxseeds

It is best to choose unsalted and unflavored if you have a choice. Roasted is fine—just watch for added oils or sugar.

A small handful of nuts or seeds per day (about 1 ounce) is perfect. They are a great, easy snack. You can also add them to yogurt or oatmeal, or sprinkled on salads.

Nuts and seeds provide the following health benefits:

- Brain health
- Joint health
- Blood sugar balance

If you have trouble chewing hard nuts or small seeds, you can eat nut butters or ground seeds.

What to Eat Less Of

Now that we've looked at what you want to include as a regular part of your diet, it's time to look at what should be reduced as a regular part of your diet. Remember, you don't have to entirely avoid them, just don't eat them more than a few times a week.

Red Meat

Red meat is considered a treat in the Mediterranean diet, not a staple. These are the foods that they eat occasionally:

1. Beef
2. Pork, lamb
3. Lamb

Red meat, especially heavily processed red meat, usually raises cholesterol, increases inflammation, and is harder on your digestive system. So, while it shouldn't be something you eat every week, you can enjoy it on occasion or in small portions, especially if you have lean cuts or they are mixed into a healthy dish.

Sugar and Sweets

Sugar has a purpose in our diets; it just isn't meant to be a main component of our diets. When eaten all of the time, processed sugars are incredibly unhealthy. Sugars contribute to a number of health issues:

- Increases inflammation
- Adds empty calories
- Spikes blood sugar
- Contributes to weight gain and fatigue

Here are the types of foods and drinks that add a lot of unnecessary sugars

- Sugary drinks
- Cookies, cakes, pastries
- Candy
- Sweetened cereals or yogurts
- Store-bought sauces or salad dressings

You can substitute all of these for healthier treats that will be a lot healthier:

- Fresh fruit when you want something sweet
- Plain yogurt with honey and fruit
- Dark chocolate (in small amounts)

You aren't giving up desserts – you're being mindful of what you are eating and choosing something that is delicious and healthy. The natural alternatives are every bit as delicious, and they won't cause a sugar rush, followed by a sugar crash.

Processed and Packaged Foods

Food that looks nothing like the original ingredients is generally not healthy. The less processed your food is, the better they are for you. For example, olive oil is made by crushing the olives – that's all that happens to them. There are no additives in the best olive oils, and that's what makes them healthy.

Heavily processed foods (which usually come in boxes and bags) often contain:

- Added sugar
- Salt
- Low-quality oils
- Preservatives
- Artificial ingredients

The following are some of the most common types of processed foods:

- Frozen dinners
- Packaged snacks (chips, crackers, granola bars)
- Sugary drinks
- Processed meats (hot dogs, sausages, deli meats)

The more these foods sneak into your diet, the more harm they do to your health. That doesn't mean you should go into your fridge and pantry to toss them out. What you should be doing is phasing them out of your diet, getting your body used to healthier foods a bit at a time.

Start simple, like changing white bread for whole wheat or flavored yogurt for plain yogurt, then add fruit to it. These are easy steps that will help you adjust your eating habits.

Hydration

The older we get, the less we notice being thirsty. Seniors may not even realize they are thirsty until they start seeing signs of dehydration, such as dizziness, fatigue, headaches, and confusion.

Staying hydrated is incredibly important:

- It supports digestion and kidney function.
- It keeps joints lubricated.
- It improves focus and energy.
- It prevents constipation.

Here are the guidelines you should try to follow more closely than the other guidelines:

- Drink 6–8 cups of water per day, more if it's hot or you're active.
- Drink herbal teas, diluted juice, or broth-based soups when you don't want just water.

Here are a few ways to increase how much you drink every day:

- Keep a water bottle nearby
- Drink with meals
- Set reminders if needed

It's best to minimize how many sugary drinks like soda or sweet tea you drink because they have a lot of sugar, which means they won't provide as much hydration.

Wine is perfectly fine, but you should drink it with food and sip it as you eat. Avoid using it to manage stress or fall asleep.

Pantry & Shopping List

The place to start making changes is with your food storage – the fridge, freezer, and pantry. What you have on hand is going to dictate what you eat, so that's where you should start as you adjust your eating habits. If you have the right ingredients readily available, it will be much easier to cook and eat healthy foods.

Remember, you don't need to clear out your pantry. This is a process of slowly replacing what you have with something better. Nor do you need to buy the most expensive and trendiest foods. What you want are local staples.

Here are the things to know and keep in mind as you go shopping, including getting the most out of your budget and reading labels without getting overwhelmed.

Essential Ingredients

The goal of adopting the Mediterranean diet is to eat fresh, healthy foods, and that means stocking your home with nourishing, versatile, and easy-to-prepare foods. Here are some of the basics to get the next time you head to the grocery store, and how you can use them.

Pantry Basics

- **Extra virgin olive oil** – Use daily for cooking, roasting, and dressings
- **Canned tomatoes** – Great for sauces, soups, and stews
- **Canned beans** (chickpeas, lentils, white beans) – Protein-rich and ready to eat
- **Brown rice, whole grain pasta, or farro** – Choose one or two to keep on hand
- **Rolled oats** – For breakfast or baking
- **Whole grain bread or crackers** – Look for simple ingredients
- **Nuts and seeds** – Almonds, walnuts, sunflower seeds (unsalted)
- **Herbs and spices** – Oregano, thyme, basil, rosemary, garlic powder, paprika

Fridge Essentials

- **Fresh vegetables** – Choose 3–5 types you enjoy
- **Fruit** – Apples, oranges, berries, or whatever's in season
- **Plain yogurt** – Use for breakfast or sauces
- **Eggs** – Great for quick meals
- **Cheese** – Feta, parmesan, or mozzarella in small amounts
- **Hummus or other bean spreads** – Easy snack or dip

Freezer Staples

- **Frozen vegetables** – Just as nutritious as fresh and very convenient
- **Frozen fruit** – For smoothies or snacks
- **Frozen fish** – Salmon, cod, or mixed seafood
- **Whole grain bread** – Freezes well and lasts longer

You can start small, replacing foods as you run out of them. Build your pantry up one shopping trip at a time, noting what you like and what you don't like. You can adjust and change what you get as you figure out what works for you.

Tips for Budget-Friendly Shopping

Eating healthy doesn't mean breaking the bank. Most of the staples of this diet, like beans, rice, and seasonal products, are easily affordable, as well as being readily available. You have to learn what you like so that you don't waste your money on foods you won't eat.

Here are a few tips for saving money when you shop.

1. Buy in Bulk (When It Makes Sense)

The staples (beans, lentils, oats, and rice) are much cheaper when you buy them in bulk. They are usually easy to store, as long as you make sure they are properly sealed after use. However, don't buy in bulk until you know that you like the food.

2. Choose Seasonal Produce

Buying fruits and vegetables in season means those foods will be much less expensive than if you buy them out of season. For example, opt for cabbage, carrots, and oranges in the winter. In the summer, look for berries, tomatoes, and zucchini. This is not only healthier, it means that you will have a built-in rotation for foods so you are far less likely to get sick of what you are eating.

3. Use Frozen and Canned Foods

Frozen vegetables and fruit are picked at their peak and often cost less than fresh foods. Canned beans, tomatoes, and fish are great for long-term storage since they last for a long time. Make sure to read the labels and opt for foods with low or no added salt or sugar.

4. Plan Before You Shop

Take the time to write a short list of what you need before you leave home. Focus on ingredients that are great in several different meals. A can of chickpeas might work in a salad one day and a stew the next.

5. Skip Processed Snacks

Something you'll realize as you start buying healthier foods is that foods like chips, cookies, and frozen dinners aren't as cheap as you may think. And you won't be able to eat as many meals with them. Skip aisles with these foods, and stock up on satisfying whole foods, like nuts, fruit, or plain yogurt—that keep you full and help you avoid impulse purchases.

Be mindful as you shop. This will not only save you money, but it will save you energy and reduce waste. With healthy ingredients readily available, you are much more likely to cook healthier meals.

How to Read Labels Simply

Labels seem to be written to overwhelm more than to inform. They have small print, lots of numbers, more complicated terms, and dubious health claims. Here are a few things to keep in mind as you look at labels.

1. Look at the Ingredient List First

The fewer ingredients a product has, the better the odds that it is healthier than the alternatives. If there are a lot of terms you don't know or a long list of ingredients, the easier it is to put it back on the shelf because you can't be sure what's actually in the food item.

2. Watch Out for Added Sugars

Even healthy products can have additives, like granola bars and flavored yogurt. Here are the words you should watch for to determine how "natural" a product is: cane sugar, honey, fructose, glucose, and syrup. If any of those are listed early (especially first), skip it.

3. Check Sodium (Salt) Content

Similarly, a lot of foods have added salt, especially nuts and seeds. Look for the salt/sodium amount on the label and make sure that it is less than 140 mg per serving. Don't get the food if the amount is higher than that.

4. Ignore Front-of-Package Claims

Words like "natural," "healthy," or "made with whole grains" don't always mean much. Ignore those labels and read the ingredient list and nutrition facts.

5. Focus on Serving Size

Many packages list numbers per "serving," not per container. If a small container has two servings and you eat the whole thing, double the numbers.

Super Simple Meal Planning

Meal planning may take a while to get used to, but it is the easiest way to make sure that you succeed in changing your habits and diet. It also takes away a lot of the stress of changing your diet. When you know what you are going to eat ahead of time, or at least have a basic idea of what you want to eat, the morning and evening won't be spent trying to come up with meals that are healthy. You'll be able to just go to the kitchen and prepare your meal.

The older we get, the more our energy fluctuates and our appetite changes. As a result, cooking often becomes more of a chore. Meal planning really helps because it provides some structure so that you can adjust your plan to suit how you are feeling when it's time to eat.

Easy Meals & No-Fuss Planning

You don't have to be rigid when you plan your meals, and you don't have to write down everything you plan to eat and compare it to what you actually eat. It's just a bit of planning to make life easier.

Decide what kind of structure works for you. Some people love to write out the meals they plan to eat a week in advance. Others prefer to have a few go-to meals and ingredients that they can choose from during the week, without having a specific day in mind. Whatever works for you is perfectly okay. The goal is to make cooking a lower-stress endeavor.

Here are a few ways to streamline the process.

- **Keep it flexible.** Plans change, and you never know when life is going to interrupt your plans. Also, you may not feel like eating something you planned to eat on a particular day, and that's fine, too. Have plans, but know that they may change. What you want is to have ideas of what you want to eat over the week, not a fixed menu.
- **Plan around your schedule.** If you tend to have more energy at a certain part of the day, plan to cook then so that it doesn't feel so much like a chore. Plan to have your easy meals ready for the times of day when you have less energy or time.
- **Repeat what works.** If you find that you love a few meals and the way they make you feel, you are more than welcome to repeat that meal a couple of times that week. It's actually great to find this out because then you can do meal prep once or twice a week, then just eat those favorite meals without having to spend a lot of time cooking the same meal a couple of times during the week.
- **Balance your meals.** Plan to have a healthy mix of vegetables, proteins, healthy fats, and whole grains. Establish a rhythm so that you can keep that healthy balance as a second nature once you get accustomed to it.

Meal planning isn't about planning every meal. It's fine to have a rough idea of what you want to eat and leave several options so that you can adjust your plan according to how you are feeling when it gets close to meal time – or when you want a quick snack.

Batch Cooking for the Week

Batch cooking is when you prepare a larger amount of food with the intention of having leftovers or to have meal prep done for a duration of time (usually a week or so in advance). This is a way of reducing the amount of time you spend cooking over the week, saving time, energy, and stress.

Consider making batch cooking a regular part of your schedule if any of these apply:

- You tire easily when cooking.
- You live alone and don't want to cook daily.
- You want to avoid daily cleanup or prep.

The following are some tips for how to make the most of your time as you batch cook:

- **One cooking session can result in two or three meals.** Choose one or two times during the week when you have the most energy. Prepare enough food to cover multiple meals. Portion what you'll eat soon and freeze the rest.
- **Start in small batch sessions to get used to it.** Don't try to make everything in one day. Even prepping just one or two meals ahead can reduce stress.
- **Think in meal parts, both the main course and sides.** You can batch-cook full meals or just components so that you spend less time cooking each day. For example, cooking a grain or a protein that can be reused across different meals makes daily prep quicker.
- **Be smart about how you store your prepped food.** Use clear containers so you can easily see what's in them. Label each container with the date, especially when you freeze the food. Store older portions at the front of the fridge so they don't go bad.

Batch cooking doesn't mean you'll be eating the same thing every day. The purpose is to simplify cooking over the week. There's something satisfying and relaxing about opening the fridge and seeing that your meal is nearly ready. It motivates you to keep eating healthy meals, even if you aren't up for cooking.

Meal Timing for Better Digestion

When you eat affects how you feel, and it affects your digestion, energy, and ability to sleep well. As you age, you are more likely to establish eating patterns that are very different from when you were younger. Small adjustments to your eating schedule can make eating more comfortable.

Here are a few tips to figure out what meal schedule works best for you.

1. **Eat at regular times.** When you skip meals, it could decrease your energy and you end up overeating later. By being consistent in when you eat, you can ensure stable energy levels and feel better.
2. **Avoid very large meals.** Eating larger portions will slow down digestion, causing you to feel bloated and fatigued. It can also lead to acid reflux. By eating lighter, more balanced meals spaced out over the day, you will avoid a lot of the discomfort associated with large meals.
3. **Give yourself time to eat.** Eating quickly may be common in today's world, but it can cause indigestion. Slow down and focus on chewing with each bite. Try to keep from being distracted or rushing through each meal.
4. **Don't eat too close to bedtime.** Sleeping after eating can cause heartburn and interrupt your sleep. Your last meal of the day should be at least two hours before bedtime.
5. **Adjust based on your appetite.** Just because you have a regular eating schedule doesn't mean you have to eat when the schedule says it's time to eat. If you aren't hungry, don't eat. If you are not very hungry, have a light snack. If you tend to go to bed early, make lunch your largest meal so that you have more time to digest before bedtime.
6. **Stay mindful of hydration.** Drink water between meals to make sure you stay hydrated. You shouldn't be drinking only when you eat meals. Drinking throughout the day improves digestion.

One of the reasons that this diet is so beneficial is that it can be tailored to you and your needs. You have to listen to your body and eat based on when you are hungry, and adjust your schedule based on your needs as you age.

Meal Variations for Specific Needs

As we age, we are more likely to have medical conditions that require changes to our dietary needs. Meal plans need to be adapted to fit those conditions. The Mediterranean diet is incredibly flexible, so making small adjustments are easy to make.

The following are the most common medical conditions and how you can modify the diet to accommodate them.

For Diabetes or Blood Sugar Control

- Emphasize fiber-rich foods: beans, lentils, oats, and non-starchy vegetables
- Choose whole grains instead of white rice or pasta
- Keep fruit portions moderate and choose low-glycemic options like berries or apples
- Pair carbohydrates with healthy fats or protein to slow absorption

Do not skip meals. This can lead to swings in your sugar level that can do a lot of harm. Plan to have smaller meals at a consistent time interval over the day to improve your energy levels and keep your blood sugar levels stable.

For Low-Sodium Needs

- Avoid processed foods and canned items with added salt
- Use herbs, spices, garlic, and lemon for flavor instead of salt
- Choose no-salt-added versions of beans, tomatoes, and broths
- Cook at home when possible, where you can control the amount of salt in a dish

When you eat cheese, cured meats, and store-bought sauces, make sure to read the labels carefully. They may have labeled the sodium in ways that make it harder to see just how much sodium is in the food, even in small amounts.

For Arthritis or Inflammation Support

1. Include anti-inflammatory foods regularly: olive oil, fatty fish, berries, leafy greens
2. Reduce processed foods and sugary snacks that may worsen joint pain
3. Limit red meat and refined flours
4. Spread several small meals out across the day to avoid large portions that can cause discomfort

Hydration is actually a very important part of reducing inflammation, so drinking water regularly over the course of the day can help reduce your pain.

Lifestyle Tips Beyond Food

The Mediterranean lifestyle isn't just about food; it's about the way you live. It affects how you move, how you think, and how you feel. This chapter focuses on three habits that support your overall well-being: moving your body, eating with awareness, and sharing meals.

Movement & Exercise for Seniors

People living around the Mediterranean Sea tend to remain more active well into old age, even though they don't go to the gym or follow any kind of exercise program. What they do is incorporate exercise into their daily routine. They walk to the market, spend time gardening, and do chores without the help of machinery. By keeping their bodies in motion over much of the day as a part of their daily habits, they don't have to create workout routines and set aside time to exercise.

There are so many ways to incorporate movement into your day. Planning for gentle, regular activity is more than enough to improve your health. Regular movements over the course of the day, instead of in one or two sessions, has several important benefits:

- Keeps joints flexible
- Maintains muscle strength
- Supports balance and prevents falls
- Improves circulation and heart health
- Boosts mood and reduces anxiety

The key to healthy movement is to make it consistent. If you can manage to get 20 to 30 minutes of light activity almost daily, you will start to see a difference in the way you feel. The following are some types of movement that could help:

- A walk after breakfast
- Light stretching in the afternoon
- Dancing to music in your living room
- Doing chores at a slower, intentional pace
- Standing up and moving every hour if you spend a lot of time sitting

Your goal is to engage your body in regular activity. Sweating and working out aren't necessary. What you want to do is to engage your body in ways that are natural, just like you are learning to eat in a more natural way.

Movement shouldn't be a chore; it should be enjoyable and feel good when you do it. If you need support to be more active, talk to your doctor or sign up for senior-friendly exercise classes.

Mindful Eating

Mediterranean meals are enjoyed and savored, not rushed. People eat slowly and deliberately, taking bites, then talking, then enjoying another bite. This relaxed attitude to meals is an incredibly healthy habit known as mindful eating.

It will probably be a real change as you start to focus on your food as you eat and not on the world around you. Pay attention to the textures, flavors, your shrinking appetite, and how your body responds.

Here are some of the benefits you'll start to notice when you practice mindful eating:

1. Improved digestion
2. Better portion control
3. Less bloating or discomfort
4. Greater enjoyment and satisfaction from meals

You'll need to be more aware of distracted eating and rushing through meals. This will be harder to stop doing if you live alone or usually eat in front of a screen. Try to eat outside occasionally. If you don't have a lawn, you can eat out on your deck or take your meal to eat on a park bench and watch the wildlife and people around you. Even sitting at a window and looking outside while you eat can help you enjoy your meal more.

Here are a few ways to start working on being more mindful as you eat:

- Sit at a table, not the couch
- Put down your fork between bites
- Chew slowly and fully
- Notice when you feel full, and stop eating gently
- Avoid multitasking while eating (TV, phone, etc.)

You don't need to think about every single bite of food because they will be pretty similar. However, you can try to keep your thoughts on the texture and other aspects, including how your body reacts.

Social Meals – The Mediterranean Way

Eating is a shared experience around the Mediterranean, making time for socializing and connecting with others. By talking and connecting,people naturally eat a lot slower. Even a simple meal is more important and meaningful when you share it with other people.

Staying connected is important, and that often becomes more difficult as we get older. Meals don't have to be complicated or formal, make them casual, enjoyable events. Here are a few ways to start building casual socialization over meals:

- Invite a neighbor for lunch
- Eat with family once a week
- Join a community meal at a center or place of worship
- Share a video call meal with someone far away

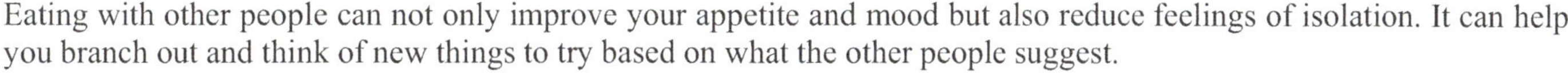

Eating with other people can not only improve your appetite and mood but also reduce feelings of isolation. It can help you branch out and think of new things to try based on what the other people suggest.

If you aren't able to make social meals every day, try to schedule time at least once a week to get accustomed to it. You could cook with someone else or go and eat out in a public place where there are other people. You may not be talking to people, but it can help you to feel more connected since you will be interacting with people at several points during the process.

Common Questions & Easy Fixes

You should always ask questions before you make a significant change, even if it is a healthy one, like switching to the Mediterranean diet. Perhaps the diet isn't complicated, but you are probably curious to know more about how it could fit into your life.

Here are a few of the most common questions, so you can start to understand how this diet could fit into your life.

"I don't like fish."

That's perfectly fine. Fish is encouraged but not mandatory since there are so many other healthy, natural sources of protein and fats. You can replace fish with the following:

- Beans, lentils, and chickpeas
- Nuts and seeds
- Olive oil
- Eggs and dairy in moderation

You can also mix small amounts of fish into other foods. With the right mix of foods, you won't even taste the fish. There are many ways to deal with an aversion or dislike of fish.

"I live alone – it's hard to cook."

Cooking for one may feel like too much work, but it doesn't have to be. You can try any of the following to make it a much easier, lower stress experience:

1. Make larger portions and refrigerate or freeze leftovers
2. Choose simple one-pan meals or soups that last for days
3. Batch prep ingredients (like grains or roasted vegetables) you can mix and match

You don't need to cook three full meals every day. Sometimes, you can batch cook once or twice a week, making meal prep very easy. Other times, you can have simple foods that add to a well-balanced meal. Meals aren't supposed to be a full, big production. They are meant to be enjoyable and relaxing.

"I'm on medications – what do I watch out for?"

Before you make any kind of change, always consult your doctor and pharmacist, especially about possible food-drug reactions. The Mediterranean diet is generally safe and beneficial, but you'll still need to be aware of potential issues.

Here are a few important things to know about foods that are important in this diet:

- Leafy greens (like spinach) can affect blood thinners.
- Grapefruit may interfere with certain medications, so make sure to ask if it's safe for your condition.
- Alcohol, even a small glass of wine, may not mix with your medications. Always check with medical professionals before you drink alcoholic beverages.

Always be informed about foods that could react badly to your condition or medications. That way you can eat well and be safe.

"I'm not used to eating so many vegetables."

That's perfectly fine, too. This isn't a diet that you should be adopting all at once. You can start by adding just one extra vegetable a day, then build up to eating more over time. If vegetables are too hard to eat, you can cook them to make them easier to chew. Over time, your taste buds will adjust, and your body will digest the roughage a little more easily.

The point is about progressing to a healthier lifestyle, not reaching perfection.

"Healthy food is expensive."

This isn't always true, especially if you purchase foods that are in season. Food staples like beans, canned tomatoes, grains, and frozen vegetables are also much more affordable. They are both affordable and rich in nutrients. Skip the packaged snacks and more expensive foods and focus on the foods you'll be able to use in multiple meals. Plan ahead so that you don't waste any of the food and to save money.

"I don't feel hungry like I used to."

That's normal because appetite changes as we age. Adjust to smaller, well-balanced meals that you can eat more often, and eat healthy snacks like yogurt, nuts, and fruits. Nutrient-rich foods give your body what you need, even if you eat them in smaller portions.

"I don't cook at all. Is this still for me?"

Yes, it is. Part of the Mediterranean diet is simple cooking. You don't need to know any complex methods of cooking because that's not how people around the Mediterranean cook their daily meals. You can start small, combining fruits, nuts, and yogurt as a snack or for breakfast, or mix canned beans with herbs and olive oil. Salads are very easy to make and are very common parts of the diet. Focus on low-sodium and pre-prepared foods as you learn basic cooking. From there, you'll be able to expand your skills and types of meals.

"How do I stay motivated?"

Starting small instead of making a lot of changes all at once is the best way to stay motivated. If it doesn't feel like a chore, it is much easier to keep going. Celebrate small wins with something you really enjoy. It won't take long before the changes themselves are the reward. Move at your own pace, and you stand a pretty good chance of succeeding.

Recipes: Real Food, Real Simple

You don't need to be a chef or a great cook to eat well. Nor do you need a lot of fancy appliances and equipment or unfamiliar ingredients. The Mediterranean diet is simple, flavorful, and nutritious, yet easy to follow.

These recipes are made specifically for seniors. Each recipe reflects the guidelines covered in the earlier chapters. Most of the meals can be made in less than 30 minutes and are easy to prepare ahead of time. The dishes are colorful and built from natural foods, not products that you get from a box or a bag.

Don't worry; you don't have to do everything from scratch. Recipes are a starting point, more like a suggestion, and you can adapt and change them as you see fit. Try the ones you think sound good and change them based on your own preferences.

Remember, keep it simple, and enjoy the process. That's what will help you enjoy your new way of eating and stay motivated.

Breakfast – Simple, senior-friendly starts

Greek Yogurt with Honey, Walnuts & Blueberries

Number of servings: 1
Preparation time: 5 minutes
Cooking time: 0 minutes

Ingredients:

- ¾ cup plain Greek yogurt (whole or low-fat)
- 1 tsp honey
- 2 tbsp chopped walnuts
- ¼ cup fresh or frozen blueberries

Directions:

1. Spoon the Greek yogurt into a bowl.
2. Drizzle with honey.
3. Top with walnuts and blueberries.
4. Serve immediately.

Nutritional value per serving: Calories: 250, Carbs: 19g, Fiber: 2g, Sugars: 11g, Protein: 15g, Saturated fat: 2g, Unsaturated fat: 8g

Difficulty rating: ★☆☆☆☆

Tips for ingredient variations: Use strawberries or raspberries instead of blueberries. Replace walnuts with almonds or sunflower seeds if preferred.

Rolled Oats with Chia Seeds, Raisins & Cinnamon

Number of servings: 1
Preparation time: 5 minutes
Cooking time: 5 minutes

Ingredients:

- ½ cup rolled oats
- 1 cup water or unsweetened almond milk
- 1 tbsp chia seeds
- 1 tbsp raisins
- ¼ tsp ground cinnamon

Directions:

1. In a small pot, bring water or almond milk to a simmer.
2. Stir in oats and cook for 4–5 minutes until soft.
3. Turn off the heat and stir in chia seeds, raisins, and cinnamon.
4. Let sit for 2–3 minutes to thicken.
5. Serve warm.

Nutritional value per serving: Calories: 220, Carbs: 35g, Fiber: 7g, Sugars: 6g, Protein: 6g, Saturated fat: 0g, Unsaturated fat: 4g

Difficulty rating: ★☆☆☆☆

Tips for ingredient variations: Add chopped apple or banana for extra sweetness. Top with a spoonful of Greek yogurt for creaminess.

Whole Grain Toast with Mashed Avocado and Olive Oil

Number of servings: 1
Preparation time: 5 minutes
Cooking time: 2 minutes

Ingredients:

- 1 slice whole grain bread
- ½ ripe avocado
- 1 tsp extra virgin olive oil
- Pinch of salt
- Pinch of black pepper

Directions:

1. Toast the slice of whole grain bread.
2. In a small bowl, mash the avocado with a fork.
3. Spread the mashed avocado over the toast.
4. Drizzle with olive oil.
5. Sprinkle with salt and pepper to taste.
6. Serve immediately.

Nutritional value per serving: Calories: 230, Carbs: 20g, Fiber: 6g, Sugars: 1g, Protein: 5g, Saturated fat: 1g, Unsaturated fat: 11g

Difficulty rating: ★☆☆☆☆

Tips for ingredient variations: Add a squeeze of lemon juice or a sprinkle of crushed red pepper. Use rye or sprouted grain bread if preferred.

Scrambled Eggs with Spinach and Cherry Tomatoes

Number of servings: 1
Preparation time: 5 minutes
Cooking time: 7 minutes

Ingredients:

- 2 eggs
- ½ cup fresh spinach, chopped
- ¼ cup cherry tomatoes, halved
- 1 tsp extra virgin olive oil
- Pinch of salt
- Pinch of black pepper

Directions:

1. Heat olive oil in a small non-stick skillet over medium heat.
2. Add spinach and cherry tomatoes. Cook for 2–3 minutes, stirring, until softened.
3. In a bowl, beat the eggs.
4. Pour the eggs into the skillet with the vegetables.
5. Stir gently and cook until eggs are set to your liking.
6. Season with salt and pepper.
7. Serve warm.

Nutritional value per serving: Calories: 210, Carbs: 4g, Fiber: 1g, Sugars: 1g, Protein: 12g, Saturated fat: 3g, Unsaturated fat: 9g

Difficulty rating: ★★☆☆☆

Tips for ingredient variations: Add fresh herbs like parsley or dill. Use kale or arugula instead of spinach if desired.

Cottage Cheese with Sliced Peaches and Slivered Almonds

Number of servings: 1
Preparation time: 5 minutes
Cooking time: 0 minutes

Ingredients:

- ½ cup low-fat cottage cheese
- ½ ripe peach, sliced thin (or use canned in water, drained)
- 1 tbsp slivered almonds

Directions:

1. Spoon the cottage cheese into a bowl.
2. Top with sliced peaches.
3. Sprinkle with slivered almonds.
4. Serve immediately.

Nutritional value per serving: Calories: 170, Carbs: 10g, Fiber: 1g, Sugars: 8g, Protein: 13g, Saturated fat: 1g, Unsaturated fat: 4g

Difficulty rating: ★☆☆☆☆

Tips for ingredient variations: Use sliced nectarines or berries instead of peaches. Swap almonds with chopped walnuts or sunflower seeds.

Boiled Eggs with Whole Grain Crackers and Cucumber

Number of servings: 1
Preparation time: 5 minutes
Cooking time: 10 minutes

Ingredients:

- 2 eggs
- 4–6 whole grain crackers
- ½ cup cucumber slices

Directions:

1. Place the eggs in a small pot and cover with cold water.
2. Bring to a boil, then lower heat and simmer for 9–10 minutes.
3. Remove eggs and cool under cold running water.
4. Peel and serve with crackers and sliced cucumber on the side.

Nutritional value per serving: Calories: 220, Carbs: 14g, Fiber: 3g, Sugars: 1g, Protein: 13g, Saturated fat: 3g, Unsaturated fat: 6g

Difficulty rating: ★☆☆☆☆

Tips for ingredient variations: Add a drizzle of olive oil and a pinch of salt to cucumber for extra flavor. Use whole grain pita chips instead of crackers if preferred.

Banana with Peanut Butter and Ground Flaxseed

Number of servings: 1

Preparation time: 5 minutes
Cooking time: 0 minutes

Ingredients:

- 1 medium banana
- 1 tbsp natural peanut butter (no added sugar)
- 1 tsp ground flaxseed

Directions:

1. Peel the banana and slice it into rounds.
2. Arrange the slices on a plate.
3. Drizzle or spread peanut butter over the banana.
4. Sprinkle with ground flaxseed.
5. Eat immediately.

Nutritional value per serving: Calories: 210, Carbs: 25g, Fiber: 4g, Sugars: 14g, Protein: 5g, Saturated fat: 1g, Unsaturated fat: 8g

Difficulty rating: ★☆☆☆☆

Tips for ingredient variations: Use almond butter instead of peanut butter. Add a pinch of cinnamon for extra flavor.

Plain Yogurt with Apple Slices and Sunflower Seeds

Number of servings: 1
Preparation time: 5 minutes
Cooking time: 0 minutes

Ingredients:

- ¾ cup plain Greek yogurt (whole or low-fat)
- ½ small apple, sliced thin
- 1 tbsp unsalted sunflower seeds

Directions:

1. Spoon the yogurt into a bowl.
2. Top with thinly sliced apple.
3. Sprinkle with sunflower seeds.
4. Serve immediately.

Nutritional value per serving: Calories: 200, Carbs: 18g, Fiber: 3g, Sugars: 10g, Protein: 12g, Saturated fat: 2g, Unsaturated fat: 6g

Difficulty rating: ★☆☆☆☆

Tips for ingredient variations: Use pear slices instead of apple. Add a drizzle of honey if you prefer a touch of sweetness.

Mediterranean Herb Omelet with Olive Oil

Number of servings: 1
Preparation time: 5 minutes
Cooking time: 6 minutes

Ingredients:

- 2 eggs
- 1 tbsp water
- 1 tsp extra virgin olive oil
- 1 tbsp chopped fresh parsley
- 1 tbsp chopped fresh dill or basil
- Pinch of salt
- Pinch of black pepper

Directions:

1. Crack the eggs into a bowl. Add water, herbs, salt, and pepper. Beat gently with a fork.
2. Heat olive oil in a small non-stick skillet over medium heat.
3. Pour in the egg mixture and let it cook undisturbed for 1–2 minutes.
4. When the edges start to set, gently lift them with a spatula and tilt the pan to let uncooked egg flow underneath.
5. Cook for another 2–3 minutes, or until fully set.
6. Fold the omelet in half and slide onto a plate. Serve warm.

Nutritional value per serving: Calories: 190, Carbs: 1g, Fiber: 0g, Sugars: 0g, Protein: 12g, Saturated fat: 3g, Unsaturated fat: 8g

Difficulty rating: ★★☆☆☆

Tips for ingredient variations: Add a spoonful of crumbled feta or chopped cherry tomatoes for extra flavor and color.

Overnight Oats with Almond Milk and Frozen Berries

Number of servings: 1
Preparation time: 5 minutes (plus overnight soak)

Cooking time: 0 minutes

Ingredients:

- ½ cup rolled oats
- ½ cup unsweetened almond milk
- ¼ cup frozen mixed berries
- 1 tbsp chia seeds
- ½ tsp cinnamon (optional)

Directions:

1. In a small jar or container, combine oats, almond milk, chia seeds, and cinnamon (if using).
2. Stir well and top with frozen berries.
3. Cover and refrigerate overnight (at least 6 hours).
4. In the morning, stir and enjoy cold or let sit at room temperature for a few minutes before eating.

Nutritional value per serving: Calories: 220, Carbs: 32g, Fiber: 7g, Sugars: 6g, Protein: 6g, Saturated fat: 0g, Unsaturated fat: 4g

Difficulty rating: ★☆☆☆☆

Tips for ingredient variations: Use fresh berries in season, or swap almond milk with oat or low-fat cow's milk. Add a few crushed walnuts for crunch.

Whole Wheat Toast with Tahini and a Drizzle of Honey

Number of servings: 1

Preparation time: 3 minutes
Cooking time: 2 minutes

Ingredients:

- 1 slice whole wheat bread
- 1 tbsp tahini
- ½ tsp honey

Directions:

1. Toast the slice of whole wheat bread to your liking.
2. Spread tahini evenly over the warm toast.
3. Drizzle lightly with honey.
4. Serve warm or at room temperature.

Nutritional value per serving: Calories: 210, Carbs: 20g, Fiber: 3g, Sugars: 4g, Protein: 5g, Saturated fat: 1g, Unsaturated fat: 9g

Difficulty rating: ★☆☆☆☆

Tips for ingredient variations: Add sliced banana or a sprinkle of cinnamon for more flavor and fiber. Use sprouted grain bread for extra nutrition.

Smoothie with Spinach, Banana, and Plain Yogurt

Number of servings: 1

Preparation time: 5 minutes
Cooking time: 0 minutes

Ingredients:

- 1 small banana
- ½ cup plain Greek yogurt
- ½ cup fresh spinach leaves
- ¼ cup water or unsweetened almond milk
- 1 tbsp ground flaxseed (optional)

Directions:

1. Place all ingredients into a blender.
2. Blend until smooth and creamy, about 30 seconds.
3. Pour into a glass and serve immediately.

Nutritional value per serving: Calories: 190, Carbs: 20g, Fiber: 4g, Sugars: 10g, Protein: 10g, Saturated fat: 2g, Unsaturated fat: 5g

Difficulty rating: ★☆☆☆☆

Tips for ingredient variations: Add a few frozen berries or a squeeze of lemon juice. Use kale or arugula instead of spinach if you like stronger greens.

Hard-Boiled Eggs with Orange Slices and Whole Grain Toast

Number of servings: 1
Preparation time: 5 minutes
Cooking time: 10 minutes

Ingredients:

- 2 eggs
- 1 orange, peeled and sliced
- 1 slice whole grain bread

Directions:

1. Place eggs in a small pot and cover with water. Bring to a boil.
2. Once boiling, reduce heat to low and simmer for 9–10 minutes.
3. Remove eggs, cool under cold running water, and peel.
4. Toast the slice of whole grain bread.
5. Arrange eggs, orange slices, and toast on a plate.
6. Serve as a balanced, protein-rich breakfast.

Nutritional value per serving: Calories: 280, Carbs: 23g, Fiber: 4g, Sugars: 9g, Protein: 13g, Saturated fat: 3g, Unsaturated fat: 6g

Difficulty rating: ★☆☆☆☆

Tips for ingredient variations: Swap the orange with apple or kiwi. Add a drizzle of olive oil or a sprinkle of paprika to the eggs for extra flavor.

Ricotta on Toast with Sliced Fresh Figs

Number of servings: 1
Preparation time: 5 minutes
Cooking time: 2 minutes

Ingredients:

- 1 slice whole grain bread
- ¼ cup ricotta cheese (low-fat or whole)
- 2 fresh figs, sliced

Directions:

1. Toast the whole grain bread until golden and crisp.
2. Spread the ricotta evenly on the toast.
3. Layer with fresh fig slices.
4. Serve immediately as a light, creamy breakfast.

Nutritional value per serving: Calories: 240, Carbs: 24g, Fiber: 4g, Sugars: 8g, Protein: 9g, Saturated fat: 3g, Unsaturated fat: 4g

Difficulty rating: ★☆☆☆☆

Tips for ingredient variations: Use pear slices or berries if figs are out of season. Add a tiny drizzle of honey or sprinkle of cinnamon for a touch of sweetness.

Warm Barley Porridge with Chopped Nuts and Dates

Number of servings: 2
Preparation time: 5 minutes
Cooking time: 20 minutes

Ingredients:

- ½ cup pearled barley
- 2 cups water
- 2 tbsp chopped dates
- 2 tbsp chopped walnuts or almonds
- ¼ tsp cinnamon (optional)

Directions:

1. Rinse the barley under cold water.
2. In a small saucepan, bring water to a boil.
3. Add barley, reduce heat to low, and simmer for 18–20 minutes until tender.
4. Stir in chopped dates and nuts.
5. Add cinnamon if desired. Let sit for 2 minutes before serving.

Nutritional value per serving: Calories: 210, Carbs: 34g, Fiber: 6g, Sugars: 6g, Protein: 5g, Saturated fat: 1g, Unsaturated fat: 6g

Difficulty rating: ★★☆☆☆

Tips for ingredient variations: Make a larger batch and reheat portions during the week. Add chopped apple or pear during cooking for more texture and fiber.

Pita with Hummus and Cucumber Rounds

Number of servings: 1
Preparation time: 5 minutes
Cooking time: 0 minutes

Ingredients:

- ½ whole wheat pita, cut into wedges
- ¼ cup hummus
- ½ small cucumber, sliced into rounds

Directions:

1. Arrange pita wedges on a small plate.
2. Spoon hummus into a small bowl or spread directly on pita.
3. Top with or serve alongside cucumber slices.
4. Enjoy as a light and refreshing Mediterranean breakfast or snack.

Nutritional value per serving: Calories: 200, Carbs: 22g, Fiber: 5g, Sugars: 2g, Protein: 6g, Saturated fat: 0g, Unsaturated fat: 6g

Difficulty rating: ★☆☆☆☆

Tips for ingredient variations: Add cherry tomatoes or olives for extra flavor. Try different hummus flavors like roasted red pepper or lemon.

Whole Grain Cereal with Milk and Sliced Strawberries

Number of servings: 1
Preparation time: 5 minutes
Cooking time: 0 minutes

Ingredients:

- ¾ cup whole grain cereal (unsweetened, high fiber)
- One can (15 oz) of rinsed and drained chickpeas
- ½ cup fresh strawberries, sliced

Directions:

1. Pour the cereal into a bowl.
2. Add milk of choice.
3. Top with sliced strawberries.
4. Serve immediately.

Nutritional value per serving: Calories: 210, Carbs: 32g, Fiber: 5g, Sugars: 8g, Protein: 8g, Saturated fat: 1g, Unsaturated fat: 3g

Difficulty rating: ★☆☆☆☆

Tips for ingredient variations: Use blueberries or banana slices instead of strawberries. Choose a cereal with at least 4g fiber and no added sugar.

Egg Muffins with Vegetables and Herbs

Number of servings: 4 (makes 4–6 muffins)
Preparation time: 10 minutes
Cooking time: 20 minutes

Ingredients:

- 4 eggs
- ½ cup chopped spinach
- ¼ cup chopped bell pepper
- 2 tbsp chopped red onion
- 1 tbsp chopped fresh parsley or basil
- 1 tbsp extra virgin olive oil
- Pinch of salt
- Pinch of black pepper

Directions:

1. Preheat oven to 375°F (190°C).
2. In a medium bowl, beat the eggs. Stir in the chopped vegetables, herbs, salt, and pepper.
3. Lightly oil a muffin tin with olive oil or use silicone liners.
4. Pour the egg mixture into 4–6 muffin cups, filling each about ¾ full.
5. Bake for 18–20 minutes or until eggs are set and lightly golden.
6. Let cool slightly before removing from the tin. Serve warm or store in the fridge for later.

Nutritional value per serving: Calories: 120, Carbs: 2g, Fiber: 0.5g, Sugars: 1g, Protein: 8g, Saturated fat: 2g, Unsaturated fat: 6g

Difficulty rating: ★★☆☆☆

Tips for ingredient variations: Swap spinach for zucchini or kale. Add a spoonful of crumbled feta for extra flavor.

Quinoa Breakfast Bowl with Yogurt and Fruit

Number of servings: 1

Preparation time: 5 minutes

Cooking time: 15 minutes (quinoa can be pre-cooked)

Ingredients:

- ½ cup cooked quinoa (cooled)
- ½ cup plain Greek yogurt
- ¼ cup sliced banana
- ¼ cup fresh or frozen watermelon
- 1 tbsp chopped almonds or walnuts
- 1 tsp honey (optional)

Directions:

1. In a bowl, layer the cooked quinoa and yogurt.
2. Top with banana slices and watermelon.
3. Sprinkle with nuts and drizzle with honey, if using.
4. Serve cold or at room temperature.

Nutritional value per serving: Calories: 260, Carbs: 28g, Fiber: 4g, Sugars: 8g, Protein: 13g, Saturated fat: 2g, Unsaturated fat: 6g

Difficulty rating: ★★☆☆☆

Tips for ingredient variations: Use chopped apples or pears in place of banana. Add cinnamon or flaxseed for extra nutrients.

Roasted Sweet Potato Slices with Tahini and Chopped Pistachios

Number of servings: 2

Preparation time: 10 minutes

Cooking time: 25 minutes

Ingredients:

- 1 medium sweet potato, peeled and sliced into ½-inch rounds
- 1 tbsp extra virgin olive oil
- 1 tbsp tahini
- 1 tbsp chopped pistachios
- Pinch of salt
- Pinch of cinnamon (optional)

Directions:

1. Preheat oven to 400°F (200°C).
2. Place sweet potato slices on a baking sheet. Brush with olive oil and sprinkle with salt.
3. Roast for 20–25 minutes, flipping halfway, until tender and lightly browned.
4. Arrange on a plate. Drizzle with tahini and sprinkle with chopped pistachios and cinnamon if using.
5. Serve warm.

Nutritional value per serving: Calories: 180, Carbs: 22g, Fiber: 4g, Sugars: 5g, Protein: 3g, Saturated fat: 1g, Unsaturated fat: 9g

Difficulty rating: ★★☆☆☆

Tips for ingredient variations: Add a spoonful of plain yogurt for a creamy finish. Use chopped walnuts or almonds instead of pistachios.

Vegetarian Mains – Meat-free Mediterranean meals

Lentil and Vegetable Stew

Number of servings: 4

Preparation time: 10 minutes

Cooking time: 25 minutes

Ingredients:

- 1 cup dry brown or green lentils
- 4 cups low-sodium vegetable broth or water
- 1 tbsp extra virgin olive oil
- 1 small onion, diced
- 2 carrots, sliced
- 1 celery stalk, chopped
- 1 zucchini, chopped
- 1 tsp dried oregano
- ½ tsp salt
- ¼ tsp black pepper
- 1 tbsp lemon juice (optional)

Directions:

1. Rinse lentils under cold water and set aside.
2. In a large pot, heat olive oil over medium heat. Add onion, carrot, and celery. Cook for 5–6 minutes until softened.
3. Add zucchini, lentils, broth or water, oregano, salt, and pepper. Bring to a boil.
4. Reduce heat and simmer uncovered for 20–25 minutes, or until lentils are tender.
5. Stir in lemon juice if using, and serve warm.

Nutritional value per serving: Calories: 240, Carbs: 35g, Fiber: 11g, Sugars: 5g, Protein: 13g, Saturated fat: 1g, Unsaturated fat: 4g

Difficulty rating: ★★☆☆☆

Tips for ingredient variations: Add spinach or kale at the end for extra greens. Use canned lentils for a quicker version—reduce cooking time accordingly.

Chickpea and Spinach Sauté with Garlic

Number of servings: 2

Preparation time: 5 minutes

Cooking time: 10 minutes

Ingredients:

- 1 can (15 oz) chickpeas, drained and rinsed
- 2 cups fresh spinach
- 2 tbsp extra virgin olive oil
- 2 garlic cloves, thinly sliced
- ¼ tsp salt
- ¼ tsp black pepper
- Pinch of red pepper flakes (optional)

Directions:

1. Heat olive oil in a skillet over medium heat. Add garlic and cook for 1–2 minutes until fragrant, but not browned.
2. Add chickpeas and sauté for 5 minutes, stirring occasionally.
3. Add spinach and cook for another 2–3 minutes until wilted.
4. Season with salt, black pepper, and red pepper flakes if using.
5. Serve warm as a light main or side dish.

Nutritional value per serving: Calories: 280, Carbs: 26g, Fiber: 8g, Sugars: 3g, Protein: 10g, Saturated fat: 1g, Unsaturated fat: 9g

Difficulty rating: ★☆☆☆☆

Tips for ingredient variations: Use kale or Swiss chard instead of spinach. Add a squeeze of lemon for brightness.

Grilled Eggplant with Tomato and Crumbled Feta

Number of servings: 2
Preparation time: 10 minutes
Cooking time: 12 minutes

Ingredients:

- 1 medium eggplant, sliced into ½-inch rounds
- 1 tbsp extra virgin olive oil
- 1 medium tomato, diced
- ¼ cup crumbled feta cheese
- ½ tsp dried oregano
- Pinch of salt and black pepper

Directions:

1. Brush eggplant slices with olive oil and sprinkle with salt, pepper, and oregano.
2. Grill or cook in a grill pan over medium heat for 5–6 minutes per side, until tender and grill-marked.
3. Place grilled eggplant on a plate. Top with diced tomato and crumbled feta.
4. Drizzle with a bit more olive oil if desired. Serve warm or at room temperature.

Nutritional value per serving: Calories: 180, Carbs: 11g, Fiber: 4g, Sugars: 6g, Protein: 5g, Saturated fat: 2g, Unsaturated fat: 8g

Difficulty rating: ★★☆☆☆

Tips for ingredient variations: Add chopped fresh parsley or basil for extra flavor. Use roasted red peppers instead of tomato for variety.

Stuffed Bell Peppers with Brown Rice, Herbs, and Olives

Number of servings: 4
Preparation time: 15 minutes
Cooking time: 30 minutes

Ingredients:

- 4 bell peppers, tops cut off and seeds removed
- 1 cup cooked brown rice
- ¼ cup chopped black olives
- ¼ cup chopped parsley
- 1 tbsp chopped fresh mint or basil
- 2 tbsp extra virgin olive oil
- 1 small tomato, chopped
- ½ tsp salt
- ¼ tsp black pepper

Directions:

1. Preheat oven to 375°F (190°C).
2. In a bowl, mix cooked brown rice, olives, parsley, mint or basil, tomato, olive oil, salt, and pepper.
3. Stuff each bell pepper with the rice mixture. Place upright in a baking dish.
4. Add a splash of water to the bottom of the dish and cover with foil.
5. Bake for 25–30 minutes, until the peppers are tender. Serve warm.

Nutritional value per serving: Calories: 220, Carbs: 28g, Fiber: 5g, Sugars: 6g, Protein: 4g, Saturated fat: 1g, Unsaturated fat: 7g

Difficulty rating: ★★☆☆☆

Tips for ingredient variations: Use quinoa or barley instead of brown rice. Add chickpeas or white beans for extra protein.

Farro Salad with Cucumber, Tomato, and Parsley

Number of servings: 4
Preparation time: 10 minutes
Cooking time: 20 minutes

Ingredients:

- 1 cup dry farro
- 2½ cups water
- 1 cup diced cucumber
- 1 cup diced tomato
- ¼ cup chopped fresh parsley
- 2 tbsp extra virgin olive oil
- 1 tbsp lemon juice
- ½ tsp salt
- ¼ tsp black pepper

Directions:

1. Rinse the farro under cold water. In a medium pot, bring water to a boil.
2. Add farro, reduce heat, and simmer for 20 minutes, or until tender. Drain and let cool slightly.
3. In a large bowl, combine cooked farro, cucumber, tomato, and parsley.
4. Drizzle with olive oil and lemon juice.
5. Season with salt and pepper. Toss gently and serve at room temperature or chilled.

Nutritional value per serving: Calories: 210, Carbs: 33g, Fiber: 5g, Sugars: 3g, Protein: 6g, Saturated fat: 0g, Unsaturated fat: 7g

Difficulty rating: ★★☆☆☆

Tips for ingredient variations: Use cherry tomatoes or add crumbled feta for a more savory version. Mint or basil can replace parsley.

White Bean and Rosemary Soup

Number of servings: 4
Preparation time: 10 minutes
Cooking time: 20 minutes

Ingredients:

- 1 tbsp extra virgin olive oil
- 1 small onion, diced
- 1 garlic clove, minced
- 2 cans (15 oz) white beans, rinsed and drained
- 3 cups low-sodium vegetable broth
- 1 tsp chopped fresh rosemary (or ½ tsp dried)
- ¼ tsp black pepper
- ¼ tsp salt (optional)

Directions:

1. In a medium pot, heat olive oil over medium heat.
2. Add onion and cook for 5 minutes, until softened.
3. Stir in garlic and rosemary; cook for 1 minute.
4. Add beans and broth. Bring to a boil, then reduce heat and simmer for 10–15 minutes.
5. Use a spoon to mash some of the beans for a creamier texture.
6. Season with salt and pepper. Serve warm.

Nutritional value per serving: Calories: 230, Carbs: 28g, Fiber: 8g, Sugars: 2g, Protein: 10g, Saturated fat: 0g, Unsaturated fat: 7g

Difficulty rating: ★★☆☆☆

Tips for ingredient variations: Add chopped spinach or kale at the end of cooking for extra greens. Use thyme instead of rosemary for a milder flavor.

Zucchini and Tomato Bake with Oregano and Olive Oil

Number of servings: 4
Preparation time: 10 minutes
Cooking time: 25 minutes

Ingredients:

- 2 medium zucchinis, sliced
- 2 medium tomatoes, sliced
- 1 small onion, thinly sliced
- 2 tbsp extra virgin olive oil
- ½ tsp dried oregano
- ¼ tsp salt
- ¼ tsp black pepper

Directions:

1. Preheat oven to 375°F (190°C).
2. In a baking dish, layer zucchini, tomato, and onion slices.
3. Drizzle with olive oil and sprinkle with oregano, salt, and pepper.
4. Cover with foil and bake for 15 minutes.
5. Uncover and bake an additional 10 minutes, or until vegetables are tender.
6. Serve warm or at room temperature.

Nutritional value per serving: Calories: 130, Carbs: 11g, Fiber: 3g, Sugars: 5g, Protein: 2g, Saturated fat: 0g, Unsaturated fat: 6g

Difficulty rating: ★★☆☆☆

Tips for ingredient variations: Add thin slices of eggplant or sprinkle with a small amount of grated parmesan before baking.

Cauliflower and Chickpea Skillet

Number of servings: 4
Preparation time: 10 minutes
Cooking time: 15 minutes

Ingredients:

- 1 tbsp extra virgin olive oil
- 1 small head cauliflower, cut into small florets
- One can (15 oz) of rinsed and drained chickpeas
- 1 garlic clove, minced
- ½ tsp ground cumin
- ½ tsp paprika
- ¼ tsp salt
- ¼ tsp black pepper
- Juice of ½ lemon

Directions:

1. Heat olive oil in a large skillet over medium heat.
2. Add cauliflower florets and cook for 5–6 minutes, stirring occasionally.
3. Add garlic, chickpeas, cumin, paprika, salt, and pepper. Stir well.
4. Cook for another 6–8 minutes until cauliflower is golden and tender.
5. Drizzle with lemon juice and serve warm.

Nutritional value per serving: Calories: 190, Carbs: 22g, Fiber: 7g, Sugars: 4g, Protein: 7g, Saturated fat: 0g, Unsaturated fat: 6g

Difficulty rating: ★★☆☆☆

Tips for ingredient variations: Add chopped fresh parsley before serving or a pinch of chili flakes for a spicy version.

Quinoa Bowl with Roasted Vegetables and Lemon Dressing

Number of servings: 2

Preparation time: 10 minutes

Cooking time: 20 minutes

Ingredients:

- ½ cup dry quinoa
- 1 cup water
- 1 cup chopped zucchini
- 1 cup chopped red bell pepper
- ½ red onion, sliced
- 1 tbsp extra virgin olive oil
- 1 tbsp lemon juice
- ¼ tsp salt
- ¼ tsp black pepper
- ½ tsp dried oregano

Directions:

1. Preheat the oven to 400°F (200°C).
2. Spread zucchini, bell pepper, and red onion on a baking sheet. Drizzle with half the olive oil, season with salt, pepper, and oregano. Roast for 20 minutes.
3. While the vegetables roast, rinse quinoa under cold water. In a small pot, bring water to a boil, add quinoa, reduce heat and simmer for 15 minutes, or until liquid is absorbed. Fluff with a fork.
4. In a bowl, combine quinoa with roasted vegetables.
5. Drizzle with remaining olive oil and lemon juice before serving.

Nutritional value per serving: Calories: 260, Carbs: 35g, Fiber: 6g, Sugars: 5g, Protein: 7g, Saturated fat: 1g, Unsaturated fat: 9g

Difficulty rating: ★★☆☆☆

Tips for ingredient variations: Add a few chickpeas or crumbled feta for extra protein. Use seasonal veggies like carrots or eggplant as alternatives.

Mushroom and Brown Rice Risotto

Number of servings: 2

Preparation time: 10 minutes

Cooking time: 25 minutes

Ingredients:

- ½ cup brown rice
- 2 cups low-sodium vegetable broth
- 1 cup sliced mushrooms (any variety)
- 1 small shallot, finely chopped
- 1 tbsp extra virgin olive oil
- 1 tbsp grated parmesan (optional)
- ¼ tsp salt
- ¼ tsp black pepper

Directions:

1. In a saucepan, heat olive oil over medium heat. Add shallot and sauté for 2 minutes.
2. Add mushrooms and cook for 5 minutes until softened.
3. Stir in brown rice and cook for 1 minute.
4. Gradually add warm broth, about ½ cup at a time, stirring frequently until absorbed before adding more. Continue until rice is tender, about 20–25 minutes.
5. Stir in parmesan (if using), and season with salt and pepper. Serve warm.

Nutritional value per serving: Calories: 240, Carbs: 36g, Fiber: 4g, Sugars: 2g, Protein: 6g, Saturated fat: 1g, Unsaturated fat: 8g

Difficulty rating: ★★☆☆☆

Tips for ingredient variations: Add peas or chopped spinach at the end for extra color and nutrients. Use barley instead of brown rice for a twist.

Baked Sweet Potato Topped with Hummus and Greens

Number of servings: 1
Preparation time: 5 minutes
Cooking time: 25 minutes

Ingredients:

- 1 medium sweet potato
- ¼ cup hummus
- ½ cup fresh arugula or baby spinach
- 1 tsp olive oil
- Pinch of salt
- Pinch of black pepper

Directions:

1. Preheat oven to 400°F (200°C).
2. Wash the sweet potato and pierce with a fork. Place on a baking sheet and bake for 25–30 minutes or until tender.
3. Once done, slice the sweet potato open. Fluff the inside with a fork.
4. Top with hummus, fresh greens, a drizzle of olive oil, and season with salt and pepper.
5. Serve warm.

Nutritional value per serving: Calories: 280, Carbs: 36g, Fiber: 6g, Sugars: 7g, Protein: 6g, Saturated fat: 1g, Unsaturated fat: 9g

Difficulty rating: ★☆☆☆☆

Tips for ingredient variations: Add a sprinkle of paprika or lemon zest. Use roasted red pepper hummus for added flavor.

Whole Grain Pasta with Sautéed Greens and Garlic

Number of servings: 2
Preparation time: 5 minutes
Cooking time: 15 minutes

Ingredients:

- 1 cup whole grain pasta
- 1 tbsp olive oil
- 2 cups chopped kale or spinach
- 2 garlic cloves, minced
- ¼ tsp salt
- ¼ tsp chili flakes (optional)
- 1 tbsp grated parmesan (optional)

Directions:

1. Cook pasta according to package instructions. Drain and set aside.
2. In a skillet, heat olive oil over medium heat. Add garlic and sauté for 1–2 minutes.
3. Add chopped greens and cook until wilted, about 3–4 minutes.
4. Toss in the cooked pasta, mix well, and season with salt and chili flakes (if using).
5. Top with parmesan if desired and serve warm.

Nutritional value per serving: Calories: 270, Carbs: 40g, Fiber: 7g, Sugars: 2g, Protein: 9g, Saturated fat: 1g, Unsaturated fat: 8g

Difficulty rating: ★☆☆☆☆

Tips for ingredient variations: Add white beans or a few cherry tomatoes for extra color and protein.

Greek-Style Baked Butter Beans (Gigantes Plaki)

Number of servings: 4
Preparation time: 10 minutes
Cooking time: 30 minutes

Ingredients:

- 2 tbsp extra virgin olive oil
- 1 small onion, diced
- 2 garlic cloves, minced
- 1 (15 oz) can butter beans (or large white beans), rinsed
- 1 (15 oz) can diced tomatoes
- 1 tsp dried oregano
- ½ tsp paprika
- Salt and pepper to taste
- ¼ cup chopped fresh parsley
- Optional: crumbled feta cheese for topping

Directions:

1. Preheat oven to 375°F (190°C).
2. Heat olive oil in a skillet over medium heat. Add onion and garlic, cook for 3–4 minutes until soft.
3. Stir in tomatoes, oregano, paprika, salt, and pepper. Simmer for 5 minutes.
4. Add butter beans and mix gently to coat.
5. Transfer everything to a small baking dish. Bake uncovered for 20–25 minutes until sauce thickens slightly.
6. Remove from oven, sprinkle with parsley (and feta if using), and serve warm.

Nutritional value per serving: Calories: 240, Carbs: 30g, Fiber: 9g, Sugars: 5g, Protein: 11g, Saturated fat: 1g, Unsaturated fat: 8g

Difficulty rating: ★★☆☆☆

Tips for ingredient variations: Use canned crushed tomatoes for a smoother texture. Add chopped spinach before baking for extra greens.

Vegetable Tagine with Chickpeas and Almonds

Number of servings: 4

Preparation time: 10 minutes

Cooking time: 25 minutes

Ingredients:

- 2 tbsp extra virgin olive oil
- 1 small onion, chopped
- 2 carrots, peeled and sliced
- 1 zucchini, sliced
- 1 red bell pepper, chopped
- 1 tsp ground cumin
- ½ tsp ground cinnamon
- ¼ tsp turmeric (optional)
- 1 (15 oz) can chickpeas, drained and rinsed
- 1 (15 oz) can diced tomatoes
- ½ cup low-sodium vegetable broth or water
- ¼ cup sliced almonds
- Salt and pepper to taste
- Fresh parsley, for garnish (optional)

Directions:

1. Heat olive oil in a large skillet or pot over medium heat.
2. Add onion and carrots. Cook for 5 minutes, stirring occasionally.
3. Add zucchini, bell pepper, cumin, cinnamon, and turmeric. Cook for 3–4 minutes until vegetables begin to soften.
4. Stir in chickpeas, diced tomatoes, and broth. Bring to a gentle simmer.
5. Cover and cook for 10–12 minutes until vegetables are tender.
6. Stir in almonds and cook for 2 more minutes.
7. Taste and season with salt and pepper.
8. Garnish with fresh parsley if desired. Serve warm.

Nutritional value per serving: Calories: 280, Carbs: 32g, Fiber: 9g, Sugars: 7g, Protein: 10g, Saturated fat: 1g, Unsaturated fat: 11g

Difficulty rating: ★★☆☆☆

Tips for ingredient variations: Swap almonds with chopped walnuts. Add raisins or dried apricots for a touch of sweetness.

Tomato and White Bean Skillet

Number of servings: 2

Preparation time: 5 minutes

Cooking time: 15 minutes

Ingredients:

- 1 tbsp extra virgin olive oil
- 1 garlic clove, minced
- 1 cup cherry tomatoes, halved
- 1 (15 oz) can white beans (cannellini or navy), rinsed
- ¼ tsp dried oregano
- Salt and black pepper to taste
- 1 tbsp chopped fresh basil or parsley (optional)

Directions:

1. Heat olive oil in a skillet over medium heat.
2. Add garlic and cook for 30 seconds, stirring gently.
3. Add cherry tomatoes and cook for 5–6 minutes until softened.
4. Add white beans and oregano. Stir and cook for another 5 minutes.
5. Season with salt and pepper to taste.
6. Garnish with chopped fresh herbs if using. Serve warm.

Nutritional value per serving: Calories: 220, Carbs: 28g, Fiber: 8g, Sugars: 4g, Protein: 10g, Saturated fat: 0g, Unsaturated fat: 7g

Difficulty rating: ★☆☆☆☆

Tips for ingredient variations: Add a handful of spinach at the end for more greens. Serve over cooked quinoa or barley for a full meal.

Fish Mains – Simple, nourishing fish-based dishes

Baked Salmon with Olive Oil and Herbs

Number of servings: 2
Preparation time: 5 minutes
Cooking time: 18 minutes

Ingredients:

- 2 salmon fillets (about 5 oz each)
- 1 tbsp extra virgin olive oil
- 1 tsp lemon juice
- ½ tsp dried oregano
- ½ tsp dried parsley
- Pinch of salt
- Pinch of black pepper

Directions:

1. Preheat the oven to 375°F (190°C).
2. Place salmon fillets on a baking dish lined with parchment paper.
3. Drizzle with olive oil and lemon juice.
4. Sprinkle with oregano, parsley, salt, and pepper.
5. Bake for 15–18 minutes, or until salmon flakes easily with a fork.
6. Serve warm, optionally with a side of steamed vegetables or whole grains.

Nutritional value per serving: Calories: 280, Carbs: 1g, Fiber: 0g, Sugars: 0g, Protein: 26g, Saturated fat: 2g, Unsaturated fat: 14g

Difficulty rating: ★★☆☆☆

Tips for ingredient variations: Use fresh herbs like dill or basil if available. Add thin lemon slices on top before baking for extra flavor.

Cod in Tomato-Olive Sauce

Number of servings: 2
Preparation time: 10 minutes
Cooking time: 15 minutes

Ingredients:

- 2 cod fillets (about 5 oz each)
- 1 tbsp extra virgin olive oil
- 1 garlic clove, minced
- 1 cup of canned diced tomatoes without salt
- ¼ cup pitted green or black olives, sliced
- 1 tsp dried oregano
- Pinch of salt
- Pinch of black pepper

Directions:

1. Heat olive oil in a skillet over medium heat. Add garlic and cook for 30 seconds.
2. Add diced tomatoes, olives, oregano, salt, and pepper. Simmer for 5 minutes.
3. Nestle cod fillets into the sauce. Cover and cook for 8–10 minutes, or until fish is opaque and flakes easily.
4. Serve warm with a side of brown rice or steamed greens.

Nutritional value per serving: Calories: 240, Carbs: 6g, Fiber: 2g, Sugars: 3g, Protein: 25g, Saturated fat: 1g, Unsaturated fat: 9g

Difficulty rating: ★★☆☆☆

Tips for ingredient variations: Use halibut or haddock in place of cod. Add a pinch of chili flakes for gentle heat.

Sardines on Whole Grain Toast with Lemon Zest

Number of servings: 1

Preparation time: 5 minutes

Cooking time: 0 minutes

Ingredients:

- 1 slice whole grain bread, toasted
- 1 can sardines in olive oil (3.75 oz), drained
- 1 tsp extra virgin olive oil (optional)
- ¼ tsp lemon zest
- Pinch of black pepper

Directions:

1. Place the toasted bread on a plate.
2. Arrange the sardines evenly on the toast.
3. Drizzle with a little extra olive oil if desired.
4. Sprinkle with lemon zest and a pinch of black pepper.
5. Serve immediately.

Nutritional value per serving: Calories: 260, Carbs: 12g, Fiber: 2g, Sugars: 1g, Protein: 21g, Saturated fat: 2g, Unsaturated fat: 13g

Difficulty rating: ★☆☆☆☆

Tips for ingredient variations: Add thin slices of tomato or arugula underneath for freshness. Use rye or sprouted grain bread if preferred.

Tuna and White Bean Salad with Parsley

Number of servings: 2

Preparation time: 10 minutes

Cooking time: 0 minutes

Ingredients:

- 1 can tuna in olive oil (5 oz), drained
- 1 cup canned white beans, rinsed and drained
- 2 tbsp chopped fresh parsley
- 1 tbsp extra virgin olive oil
- 1 tbsp lemon juice
- ¼ tsp salt
- ¼ tsp black pepper

Directions:

1. In a medium bowl, combine tuna and white beans.
2. Add parsley, olive oil, and lemon juice.
3. Season with salt and pepper.
4. Toss gently to combine.
5. Serve chilled or at room temperature.

Nutritional value per serving: Calories: 260, Carbs: 14g, Fiber: 4g, Sugars: 1g, Protein: 20g, Saturated fat: 1g, Unsaturated fat: 11g

Difficulty rating: ★☆☆☆☆

Tips for ingredient variations: Add chopped celery or red onion for crunch. Use cannellini or great northern beans for best texture.

Grilled Trout with Garlic and Lemon

Number of servings: 2

Preparation time: 10 minutes

Cooking time: 10 minutes

Ingredients:

- 2 small whole trout, cleaned and gutted (or 2 trout fillets)
- 1 tbsp extra virgin olive oil
- 2 cloves garlic, finely chopped
- 1 lemon, sliced
- ½ tsp salt
- ¼ tsp black pepper
- Fresh parsley for garnish (optional)

Directions:

1. Preheat a grill or stovetop grill pan to medium-high heat.
2. Pat the trout dry and rub both sides with olive oil.
3. Sprinkle with salt, pepper, and chopped garlic.
4. Place a few lemon slices inside the cavity (if using whole trout) or on top of the fillets.
5. Grill for 4–5 minutes per side, or until the fish is opaque and flakes easily with a fork.
6. Garnish with fresh parsley and serve with a squeeze of lemon juice.

Nutritional value per serving: Calories: 290, Carbs: 3g, Fiber: 1g, Sugars: 0g, Protein: 30g, Saturated fat: 2g, Unsaturated fat: 10g

Difficulty rating: ★★☆☆☆

Tips for ingredient variations: Use cod or salmon if trout isn't available. Add thin zucchini slices to the grill for a complete meal.

Mediterranean Fish Stew with Tomatoes and Potatoes

Number of servings: 4

Preparation time: 10 minutes

Cooking time: 25 minutes

Ingredients:

- 1 tbsp extra virgin olive oil
- 1 small onion, chopped
- 2 garlic cloves, minced
- 2 medium potatoes, peeled and diced
- 1 (14 oz) can diced tomatoes (no salt added)
- 2 cups low-sodium vegetable or fish broth
- ¾ lb firm white fish (like cod or haddock), cut into chunks
- ½ tsp dried oregano
- ½ tsp salt
- ¼ tsp black pepper
- 2 tbsp chopped fresh parsley

Directions:

1. In a large pot, heat olive oil over medium heat.
2. Add onion and garlic; cook for 3–4 minutes until softened.
3. Stir in potatoes, tomatoes, broth, oregano, salt, and pepper.
4. Bring to a boil, then reduce heat and simmer for 15–18 minutes, until potatoes are tender.
5. Add fish and simmer gently for another 5–7 minutes, or until fish is fully cooked.
6. Sprinkle with parsley and serve warm.

Nutritional value per serving: Calories: 250, Carbs: 22g, Fiber: 4g, Sugars: 4g, Protein: 20g, Saturated fat: 1g, Unsaturated fat: 7g

Difficulty rating: ★★☆☆☆

Tips for ingredient variations: Add chopped zucchini or spinach near the end of cooking for extra color and nutrition.

Salmon Patties with Yogurt Dill Sauce

Number of servings: 4 (makes 4 patties)

Preparation time: 10 minutes

Cooking time: 10 minutes

Ingredients:

- 1 (14 oz) can wild-caught salmon, drained
- 1 egg
- ¼ cup whole wheat breadcrumbs or oats
- 1 tbsp plain Greek yogurt
- 1 tbsp chopped fresh dill or 1 tsp dried
- 1 tsp lemon juice
- 1 tbsp extra virgin olive oil (for cooking)

Yogurt Dill Sauce:

- ¼ cup plain Greek yogurt
- 1 tsp lemon juice
- 1 tsp chopped fresh dill
- Pinch of salt

Directions:

1. In a bowl, mix salmon, egg, breadcrumbs, yogurt, dill, and lemon juice until combined.
2. Form into 4 equal patties.
3. Heat olive oil in a skillet over medium heat.
4. Cook patties for 4–5 minutes per side, or until golden and firm.
5. In a small bowl, mix the sauce ingredients.
6. Serve patties warm with a spoonful of yogurt dill sauce on top.

Nutritional value per serving: Calories: 270, Carbs: 6g, Fiber: 1g, Sugars: 1g, Protein: 25g, Saturated fat: 2g, Unsaturated fat: 9g

Difficulty rating: ★★☆☆☆

Tips for ingredient variations: Add finely chopped spinach or parsley to the patties for extra greens. Can be made in advance and reheated.

Broiled Mackerel with Lemon

Number of servings: 2

Preparation time: 5 minutes

Cooking time: 10 minutes

Ingredients:

- 2 mackerel fillets (skin on)
- 1 tbsp extra virgin olive oil
- 1 clove garlic, minced
- Juice of ½ lemon
- ½ tsp dried thyme or oregano
- Pinch of salt
- Pinch of black pepper

Directions:

1. Preheat broiler to high. Line a baking tray with foil or parchment paper.
2. In a small bowl, mix olive oil, garlic, lemon juice, thyme, salt, and pepper.
3. Place mackerel fillets on the tray, skin side down.
4. Brush the fillets evenly with the oil mixture.
5. Broil for 8–10 minutes, or until the fish is golden and flakes easily.
6. Serve warm with extra lemon wedges if desired.

Nutritional value per serving: Calories: 290, Carbs: 1g, Fiber: 0g, Sugars: 0g, Protein: 27g, Saturated fat: 3g, Unsaturated fat: 11g

Difficulty rating: ★☆☆☆☆

Tips for ingredient variations: Add sliced tomatoes or red onions under the fish for extra flavor and moisture.

Baked Tilapia with Cherry Tomatoes

Number of servings: 2

Preparation time: 10 minutes

Cooking time: 15 minutes

Ingredients:

- 2 tilapia fillets (about 4 oz each)
- 1 cup cherry tomatoes, halved
- 1 tbsp extra virgin olive oil
- 1 garlic clove, minced
- ½ tsp dried oregano
- ¼ tsp salt
- ¼ tsp black pepper
- Juice of ½ lemon

Directions:

1. Preheat oven to 375°F (190°C).
2. Place the tilapia fillets in a small baking dish.
3. In a bowl, toss cherry tomatoes with olive oil, garlic, oregano, salt, and pepper.
4. Pour the tomato mixture over the fish.
5. Squeeze lemon juice over everything.
6. Bake for 12–15 minutes, or until the fish flakes easily with a fork.
7. Serve warm, spooning tomatoes and juices over the fillets.

Nutritional value per serving: Calories: 220, Carbs: 5g, Fiber: 1g, Sugars: 2g, Protein: 26g, Saturated fat: 1g, Unsaturated fat: 9g

Difficulty rating: ★★☆☆☆

Tips for ingredient variations: Use cod or haddock instead of tilapia. Add chopped olives or capers for extra flavor.

Tuna-Stuffed Tomatoes with Capers

Number of servings: 2
Preparation time: 10 minutes
Cooking time: 0 minutes
Ingredients:

- 2 medium ripe tomatoes
- 1 (5 oz) can tuna packed in olive oil, drained
- 1 tbsp capers, rinsed and chopped
- 1 tbsp chopped parsley
- 1 tbsp plain Greek yogurt
- ¼ tsp black pepper
- Pinch of salt (optional)

Directions:

1. Cut off the tomato tops, then use a spoon to remove the pulp and seeds.
2. In a bowl, mix tuna, capers, parsley, yogurt, pepper, and salt (if needed).
3. Stuff the tomato shells with the tuna mixture.
4. Chill for 10 minutes or serve immediately.

Nutritional value per serving: Calories: 200, Carbs: 5g, Fiber: 2g, Sugars: 3g, Protein: 20g, Saturated fat: 1g, Unsaturated fat: 10g

Difficulty rating: ★☆☆☆☆

Tips for ingredient variations: Replace yogurt with mashed avocado for a dairy-free option. Add chopped celery for crunch.

Fish and Lentil Soup with Fresh Herbs

Number of servings: 4
Preparation time: 10 minutes
Cooking time: 25 minutes
Ingredients:

- 1 tbsp extra virgin olive oil
- 1 small onion, chopped
- 1 carrot, diced
- 1 celery stalk, diced
- 1 garlic clove, minced
- ½ cup dry green or brown lentils, rinsed
- 4 cups low-sodium vegetable or fish broth
- 2 white fish fillets (tilapia or cod), cut into chunks
- 2 tbsp chopped fresh parsley
- Salt and pepper to taste

Directions:

1. In a large pot, heat olive oil over medium heat.
2. Add onion, carrot, and celery. Cook for 5 minutes, stirring occasionally.
3. Add garlic and lentils. Stir for 1 minute.
4. Pour in the broth and bring to a boil. Reduce heat and simmer for 15–18 minutes, until lentils are tender.
5. Add the fish pieces and simmer for another 5–7 minutes, until fish is cooked through.
6. Stir in parsley, season with salt and pepper, and serve hot.

Nutritional value per serving: Calories: 260, Carbs: 20g, Fiber: 6g, Sugars: 4g, Protein: 22g, Saturated fat: 1g, Unsaturated fat: 6g

Difficulty rating: ★★☆☆☆

Tips for ingredient variations: Use salmon or trout instead of white fish. Add a squeeze of lemon juice before serving.

Shrimp Sautéed with Garlic and Greens

Number of servings: 2
Preparation time: 10 minutes
Cooking time: 8 minutes
Ingredients:

- 1 tbsp extra virgin olive oil
- 2 garlic cloves, sliced
- 8 oz peeled shrimp (medium size)
- 2 cups fresh spinach or chopped kale
- ¼ tsp salt
- ¼ tsp red pepper flakes (optional)
- Juice of ½ lemon

Directions:

1. Heat olive oil in a large skillet over medium heat.
2. Add garlic and sauté for 1 minute until fragrant.
3. Add shrimp and cook for 2–3 minutes per side until pink and opaque.
4. Add greens, salt, and red pepper flakes (if using). Stir and cook for 2–3 more minutes until wilted.
5. Squeeze lemon juice over the top and serve warm.

Nutritional value per serving: Calories: 210, Carbs: 3g, Fiber: 1g, Sugars: 0g, Protein: 24g, Saturated fat: 1g, Unsaturated fat: 9g

Difficulty rating: ★★☆☆☆

Tips for ingredient variations: Use arugula or Swiss chard instead of spinach. Add cherry tomatoes for a touch of sweetness.

Tuna and Quinoa Cakes

Number of servings: 2 (makes 4 small cakes)
Preparation time: 10 minutes
Cooking time: 10 minutes

Ingredients:

- 1 can (5 oz) tuna in olive oil, drained
- ¾ cup cooked quinoa
- 1 egg
- 1 tbsp chopped parsley
- 1 tbsp chopped green onion
- ¼ tsp garlic powder
- ¼ tsp salt
- ¼ tsp black pepper
- 1 tsp olive oil (for cooking)

Directions:

1. In a bowl, combine tuna, cooked quinoa, egg, parsley, green onion, garlic powder, salt, and pepper. Mix well.
2. Form mixture into 4 small patties using your hands or a spoon.
3. Heat olive oil in a non-stick skillet over medium heat.
4. Cook patties for 3–4 minutes on each side until golden brown and firm.
5. Serve warm with a green salad or steamed vegetables.

Nutritional value per serving: Calories: 250, Carbs: 12g, Fiber: 2g, Sugars: 1g, Protein: 22g, Saturated fat: 2g, Unsaturated fat: 9g

Difficulty rating: ★★☆☆☆

Tips for ingredient variations: Use canned salmon instead of tuna, or add a bit of lemon zest for extra brightness.

Cold Salmon Salad with Cucumber and Yogurt Dressing

Number of servings: 2
Preparation time: 10 minutes
Cooking time: 10 minutes (if cooking salmon fresh)

Ingredients:

- 1 cup cooked salmon (cooled) or 1 packet (5 oz) smoked salmon
- 1 small cucumber, thinly sliced
- 2 cups mixed greens or arugula
- ¼ cup plain Greek yogurt
- 1 tbsp lemon juice
- 1 tbsp chopped fresh dill
- 1 tsp olive oil
- Pinch of salt and pepper

Directions:

1. In a small bowl, mix yogurt, lemon juice, dill, olive oil, salt, and pepper to make the dressing.
2. In a serving bowl, toss together mixed greens and cucumber.
3. Top with flaked or sliced salmon.
4. Drizzle with yogurt dressing and serve cold.

Nutritional value per serving: Calories: 230, Carbs: 6g, Fiber: 2g, Sugars: 3g, Protein: 20g, Saturated fat: 2g, Unsaturated fat: 8g

Difficulty rating: ★☆☆☆☆

Tips for ingredient variations: Add sliced radishes or capers. Swap dill with parsley if preferred.

Foil-Baked Cod with Zucchini and Lemon

Number of servings: 2
Preparation time: 10 minutes
Cooking time: 15 minutes

Ingredients:

- 2 cod fillets (4–5 oz each)
- 1 small zucchini, sliced into thin rounds
- 1 tbsp olive oil
- 1 tbsp lemon juice
- ½ tsp dried oregano
- Salt and pepper to taste
- 2 lemon slices (optional)

Directions:

1. Preheat oven to 375°F (190°C).
2. On a baking sheet, place two pieces of aluminum foil.
3. On each piece, lay half of the zucchini slices, top with a cod fillet.
4. Drizzle with olive oil and lemon juice, then sprinkle with oregano, salt, and pepper. Add a lemon slice on top if using.
5. Fold foil to create a sealed packet.
6. Bake for 15 minutes or until fish flakes easily with a fork.
7. Carefully open packets and serve directly or transfer to a plate.

Nutritional value per serving: Calories: 210, Carbs: 5g, Fiber: 1g, Sugars: 2g, Protein: 25g, Saturated fat: 1g, Unsaturated fat: 7g

Difficulty rating: ★★☆☆☆

Tips for ingredient variations: Use summer squash instead of zucchini. Add cherry tomatoes or olives for extra flavor.

Tuna, Chickpea, and Arugula Bowl

Number of servings: 2
Preparation time: 10 minutes
Cooking time: 0 minutes

Ingredients:

- 1 can (5 oz) tuna in olive oil, drained
- 1 cup canned chickpeas, rinsed and drained
- 2 cups fresh arugula
- ¼ cup cherry tomatoes, halved
- 2 tbsp extra virgin olive oil
- 1 tbsp lemon juice
- Pinch of salt and pepper

Directions:

1. In a medium bowl, combine tuna and chickpeas.
2. In a separate small bowl, whisk together olive oil, lemon juice, salt, and pepper.
3. Place arugula and cherry tomatoes in serving bowls.
4. Top with the tuna-chickpea mix.
5. Drizzle with dressing and serve immediately.

Nutritional value per serving: Calories: 290, Carbs: 14g, Fiber: 5g, Sugars: 2g, Protein: 22g, Saturated fat: 2g, Unsaturated fat: 12g

Difficulty rating: ★☆☆☆☆

Tips for ingredient variations: Replace arugula with baby spinach. Add thinly sliced red onion or olives for more flavor.

Grilled Swordfish with Lemon and Herbs

Number of servings: 2
Preparation time: 10 minutes
Cooking time: 10 minutes

Ingredients:

- 2 swordfish steaks (about 4–6 oz each)
- 1 tbsp extra virgin olive oil
- Juice of ½ lemon
- 1 tsp chopped fresh parsley
- ½ tsp dried oregano
- ¼ tsp salt
- ¼ tsp black pepper

Directions:

1. Preheat a grill or grill pan over medium-high heat.
2. In a small bowl, mix olive oil, lemon juice, parsley, oregano, salt, and pepper.
3. Brush the swordfish steaks with the mixture on both sides.
4. Grill the swordfish for 4–5 minutes per side, or until cooked through and slightly charred.
5. Transfer to a plate and drizzle with any remaining dressing. Serve warm.

Nutritional value per serving: Calories: 280, Carbs: 1g, Fiber: 0g, Sugars: 0g, Protein: 30g, Saturated fat: 2g, Unsaturated fat: 10g

Difficulty rating: ★★☆☆☆

Tips for ingredient variations: Use fresh basil or thyme instead of parsley. Add a few capers or olives on the side for extra flavor.

Baked Haddock with Capers and Olive Oil

Number of servings: 2
Preparation time: 5 minutes
Cooking time: 15 minutes

Ingredients:

- 2 haddock fillets (about 5 oz each)
- 1 tbsp extra virgin olive oil
- 1 tbsp lemon juice
- 1 tbsp capers, rinsed
- ¼ tsp salt
- ¼ tsp black pepper

Directions:

1. Preheat the oven to 375°F (190°C).
2. Place the haddock fillets in a baking dish.
3. Drizzle with olive oil and lemon juice.
4. Sprinkle with capers, salt, and pepper.
5. Bake for 12–15 minutes, or until the fish flakes easily with a fork.
6. Serve with steamed vegetables or a grain side.

Nutritional value per serving: Calories: 200, Carbs: 1g, Fiber: 0g, Sugars: 0g, Protein: 25g, Saturated fat: 1g, Unsaturated fat: 8g

Difficulty rating: ★☆☆☆☆

Tips for ingredient variations: Use cod or tilapia if haddock is unavailable. Add thinly sliced zucchini or tomatoes to the baking dish.

Smoked Salmon on Rye Toast with Dill

Number of servings: 1
Preparation time: 5 minutes
Cooking time: 2 minutes

Ingredients:

- 1 slice rye or whole grain bread
- 2 oz smoked salmon
- 1 tsp extra virgin olive oil
- 1 tsp chopped fresh dill
- ½ tsp lemon juice
- Optional: a few thin cucumber slices

Directions:

1. Toast the rye bread to your liking.
2. Top with smoked salmon and drizzle with olive oil and lemon juice.
3. Sprinkle with fresh dill.
4. Add cucumber slices if using, and serve immediately.

Nutritional value per serving: Calories: 230, Carbs: 15g, Fiber: 3g, Sugars: 1g, Protein: 14g, Saturated fat: 1g, Unsaturated fat: 9g

Difficulty rating: ★☆☆☆☆

Tips for ingredient variations: Use plain Greek yogurt as a spread base. Substitute dill with chives or parsley.

Pasta with Tuna, Olives, and Parsley

Number of servings: 2
Preparation time: 10 minutes
Cooking time: 12 minutes

Ingredients:

- 4 oz whole wheat pasta (such as penne or fusilli)
- 1 can tuna in olive oil (5 oz), drained
- 2 tbsp chopped parsley
- 2 tbsp sliced black or green olives
- 1 tbsp extra virgin olive oil
- 1 clove garlic, minced
- ¼ tsp salt
- ¼ tsp black pepper

Directions:

1. Pasta should be cooked in boiling water as directed on the package. Drain and set aside.
2. In a large pan, heat olive oil over medium heat. Add garlic and cook for 1 minute.
3. Add drained tuna and olives. Stir gently for 2 minutes.
4. Add the cooked pasta and toss to combine.
5. Sprinkle with parsley, season with salt and pepper, and serve warm.

Nutritional value per serving: Calories: 340, Carbs: 28g, Fiber: 5g, Sugars: 1g, Protein: 20g, Saturated fat: 1g, Unsaturated fat: 10g

Difficulty rating: ★★☆☆☆

Tips for ingredient variations: Add halved cherry tomatoes or a few capers. For more vegetables, stir in cooked spinach or zucchini.

Sardines and White Bean Mash on Toast

Number of servings: 2
Preparation time: 10 minutes
Cooking time: 5 minutes

Ingredients:

- 1 can (3.75 oz) sardines in olive oil, drained
- 1 cup canned white beans, rinsed and drained
- 1 tbsp extra virgin olive oil
- 1 tsp lemon juice
- Pinch of salt
- Pinch of black pepper
- 2 slices whole grain bread

Directions:

1. In a small bowl, mash the white beans with olive oil, lemon juice, salt, and pepper until smooth but slightly chunky.
2. Toast the bread slices to your liking.
3. Spread the white bean mash onto the toast.
4. Top with sardines, breaking them slightly to distribute evenly.
5. Serve warm or at room temperature.

Nutritional value per serving: Calories: 280, Carbs: 24g, Fiber: 5g, Sugars: 1g, Protein: 17g, Saturated fat: 2g, Unsaturated fat: 10g

Difficulty rating: ★☆☆☆☆

Tips for ingredient variations: Add chopped parsley or a sprinkle of paprika. Use rye or multigrain toast for variety.

Halibut Baked with Cherry Tomatoes and Onions

Number of servings: 2

Preparation time: 10 minutes

Cooking time: 15 minutes

Ingredients:

- 2 halibut fillets (4–5 oz each)
- 1 cup cherry tomatoes, halved
- ½ small red onion, thinly sliced
- 1 tbsp extra virgin olive oil
- ½ tsp dried oregano
- ¼ tsp salt
- ¼ tsp black pepper

Directions:

1. Preheat oven to 375°F (190°C).
2. Place halibut fillets in a baking dish. Scatter cherry tomatoes and onion slices around the fish.
3. Drizzle everything with olive oil and sprinkle with oregano, salt, and pepper.
4. Bake for 12–15 minutes, or until fish flakes easily with a fork.
5. Serve warm with steamed vegetables or whole grains.

Nutritional value per serving: Calories: 260, Carbs: 6g, Fiber: 1g, Sugars: 3g, Protein: 28g, Saturated fat: 1g, Unsaturated fat: 9g

Difficulty rating: ★★☆☆☆

Tips for ingredient variations: Substitute halibut with cod or haddock. Add a few olives or capers for extra flavor.

Poached Salmon with Dill and Lemon

Number of servings: 2

Preparation time: 5 minutes

Cooking time: 12 minutes

Ingredients:

- 2 salmon fillets (4 oz each)
- 2 cups water
- 2 slices lemon
- 2 sprigs fresh dill (or ½ tsp dried dill)
- Pinch of salt

Directions:

1. In a shallow saucepan, bring water, lemon slices, dill, and salt to a gentle simmer.
2. Add salmon fillets, skin-side down, making sure they're mostly submerged.
3. Cover and simmer gently for 10–12 minutes, or until salmon is opaque and flakes easily.
4. Remove with a spatula and serve warm or chilled.

Nutritional value per serving: Calories: 210, Carbs: 0g, Fiber: 0g, Sugars: 0g, Protein: 23g, Saturated fat: 2g, Unsaturated fat: 8g

Difficulty rating: ★★☆☆☆

Tips for ingredient variations: Serve with a spoonful of plain yogurt mixed with lemon zest and dill. Great over a bed of greens.

Anchovy and Tomato Whole Grain Flatbread

Number of servings: 2

Preparation time: 10 minutes

Cooking time: 10 minutes

Ingredients:

- 1 whole grain flatbread or pita (8-inch)
- 4 anchovy fillets, chopped
- ½ cup cherry tomatoes, halved
- 1 tbsp extra virgin olive oil
- ¼ tsp dried oregano
- ¼ tsp black pepper

Directions:

1. Preheat oven to 375°F (190°C).
2. Place the flatbread on a baking sheet. Top with cherry tomatoes and chopped anchovies.
3. Drizzle with olive oil and sprinkle with oregano and black pepper.
4. Bake for 8–10 minutes, or until edges are crisp and tomatoes are softened.
5. Cut and serve warm.

Nutritional value per serving: Calories: 220, Carbs: 22g, Fiber: 3g, Sugars: 2g, Protein: 9g, Saturated fat: 1g, Unsaturated fat: 7g

Difficulty rating: ★☆☆☆☆

Tips for ingredient variations: Add sliced olives or a sprinkle of grated Parmesan. Use a whole wheat tortilla if flatbread isn't available.

Mussels in a Light Tomato Broth with Herbs

Number of servings: 2

Preparation time: 10 minutes

Cooking time: 10 minutes

Ingredients:

- 1 lb mussels, cleaned and debearded
- 1 tbsp extra virgin olive oil
- 2 garlic cloves, minced
- ½ cup cherry tomatoes, halved
- ½ cup low-sodium vegetable broth or water
- 2 tbsp chopped fresh parsley
- ¼ tsp chili flakes (optional)

Directions:

1. Heat olive oil in a large pot over medium heat. Add garlic and cook for 30 seconds.
2. Add cherry tomatoes and cook for 2–3 minutes, until softened.
3. Pour in broth and bring to a simmer.
4. Cover, add mussels, and cook until mussels open, 5 to 7 minutes. Throw away any that don't.
5. Sprinkle with parsley and serve with whole grain bread to soak up the broth.

Nutritional value per serving: Calories: 220, Carbs: 7g, Fiber: 2g, Sugars: 2g, Protein: 20g, Saturated fat: 1g, Unsaturated fat: 7g

Difficulty rating: ★★☆☆☆

Tips for ingredient variations: Add a splash of lemon juice or white wine during cooking. Use canned diced tomatoes if cherry tomatoes aren't available.

Chicken Mains – Mediterranean chicken dishes

Lemon and Rosemary Baked Chicken Thighs

Number of servings: 4

Preparation time: 10 minutes

Cooking time: 25 minutes

Ingredients:

- 4 boneless, skinless chicken thighs
- 2 tbsp extra virgin olive oil
- Juice of 1 lemon
- 1 tsp fresh rosemary, chopped (or ½ tsp dried)
- 1 clove garlic, minced
- ½ tsp salt
- ¼ tsp black pepper

Directions:

1. Preheat oven to 400°F (200°C).
2. In a small bowl, whisk together olive oil, lemon juice, rosemary, garlic, salt, and pepper.
3. Place chicken thighs in a baking dish and pour the mixture over them.
4. Toss to coat, then spread the thighs evenly in the dish.
5. Bake for 25 minutes or until cooked through and lightly golden.
6. Let rest for 5 minutes before serving.

Nutritional value per serving: Calories: 250, Carbs: 1g, Fiber: 0g, Sugars: 0g, Protein: 24g, Saturated fat: 3g, Unsaturated fat: 10g

Difficulty rating: ★★☆☆☆

Tips for ingredient variations: Add sliced red onions or cherry tomatoes to the baking dish for extra color and flavor.

Chicken Stir-Fry with Seasonal Vegetables and Olive Oil

Number of servings: 2

Preparation time: 10 minutes

Cooking time: 12 minutes

Ingredients:

- 1 medium boneless, skinless chicken breast, sliced thin
- 1 tbsp extra virgin olive oil
- 1 small zucchini, sliced
- ½ red bell pepper, sliced
- 1 cup broccoli florets
- 1 clove garlic, minced
- Pinch of salt
- Pinch of black pepper

Directions:

1. Heat olive oil in a large skillet over medium heat.
2. Add chicken slices and cook for 4–5 minutes until browned. Remove and set aside.
3. In the same pan, add garlic and vegetables. Cook for 5–6 minutes, stirring occasionally, until just tender.
4. Return chicken to the pan, stir to combine, and cook for 2 more minutes.
5. Season with salt and pepper and serve warm.

Nutritional value per serving: Calories: 280, Carbs: 8g, Fiber: 3g, Sugars: 4g, Protein: 26g, Saturated fat: 2g, Unsaturated fat: 9g

Difficulty rating: ★★☆☆☆

Tips for ingredient variations: Use whatever vegetables are in season—carrots, snap peas, spinach, or mushrooms work well too.

Stewed Chicken with Chickpeas and Tomato

Number of servings: 4

Preparation time: 10 minutes

Cooking time: 25 minutes

Ingredients:

- 2 medium boneless, skinless chicken breasts, diced
- 1 tbsp extra virgin olive oil
- 1 can (15 oz) no-salt-added chickpeas, rinsed
- 1 cup canned diced tomatoes (no added salt)
- ½ cup water
- ½ tsp ground cumin
- ½ tsp paprika
- ¼ tsp salt
- ¼ tsp black pepper

Directions:

1. Heat olive oil in a large saucepan over medium heat.
2. Add chicken and cook for 5–6 minutes, until lightly browned.
3. Stir in chickpeas, tomatoes, water, cumin, paprika, salt, and pepper.
4. Bring to a simmer, cover, and cook for 15–20 minutes, stirring occasionally.
5. Serve warm, optionally with a slice of whole grain bread or over brown rice.

Nutritional value per serving: Calories: 310, Carbs: 16g, Fiber: 5g, Sugars: 3g, Protein: 27g, Saturated fat: 2g, Unsaturated fat: 7g

Difficulty rating: ★★☆☆☆

Tips for ingredient variations: Add chopped spinach or kale in the last 5 minutes of cooking for extra greens.

Grilled Chicken Breast with Mediterranean Herb Rub

Number of servings: 2

Preparation time: 10 minutes

Cooking time: 15 minutes

Ingredients:

- 2 small boneless, skinless chicken breasts
- 1 tbsp extra virgin olive oil
- 1 tsp dried oregano
- ½ tsp dried thyme
- ½ tsp garlic powder
- Zest of ½ lemon
- ¼ tsp salt
- ¼ tsp black pepper

Directions:

1. In a small bowl, mix olive oil, oregano, thyme, garlic powder, lemon zest, salt, and pepper to form a paste.
2. Rub mixture evenly over both chicken breasts.
3. Preheat grill or grill pan to medium heat.
4. Grill chicken for 6–8 minutes per side, or until cooked through and grill marks appear.
5. Let rest for 5 minutes before slicing and serving.

Nutritional value per serving: Calories: 240, Carbs: 1g, Fiber: 0g, Sugars: 0g, Protein: 28g, Saturated fat: 2g, Unsaturated fat: 8g

Difficulty rating: ★★☆☆☆

Tips for ingredient variations: Serve with a side of steamed vegetables or a small whole grain salad.

Chicken and Lentil One-Pan Meal

Number of servings: 4

Preparation time: 10 minutes

Cooking time: 25 minutes

Ingredients:

- 1 tbsp extra virgin olive oil
- 1 small yellow onion, chopped
- 1 garlic clove, minced
- 1 cup dry green or brown lentils, rinsed
- 2 boneless, skinless chicken breasts, cut into chunks
- 2 cups low-sodium vegetable or chicken broth
- 1 tsp dried thyme or oregano
- 1 cup chopped spinach or kale
- Salt and black pepper to taste

Directions:

1. Heat olive oil in a large skillet over medium heat.
2. Add onion and garlic, and sauté for 2–3 minutes until softened.
3. Stir in the lentils and mix for 1 minute.
4. Add chicken, broth, and thyme. Bring to a low boil.
5. Cover and simmer for 20–25 minutes, until lentils are tender and chicken is fully cooked.
6. Stir in spinach during the last 5 minutes of cooking.
7. Season with salt and pepper before serving.

Nutritional value per serving: Calories: 310, Carbs: 24g, Fiber: 7g, Sugars: 2g, Protein: 28g, Saturated fat: 1g, Unsaturated fat: 7g

Difficulty rating: ★★☆☆☆

Tips for ingredient variations: Use canned lentils to save time (reduce broth amount). Add chopped carrots or zucchini for more vegetables.

Olive Oil Roasted Chicken with Oregano and Lemon

Number of servings: 4

Preparation time: 10 minutes

Cooking time: 30 minutes

Ingredients:

- 4 skinless chicken thighs or drumsticks
- 2 tbsp extra virgin olive oil
- Juice of 1 lemon
- 1 tbsp dried oregano
- 2 garlic cloves, minced
- ½ tsp salt
- ¼ tsp black pepper

Directions:

1. Preheat oven to 400°F (200°C).
2. In a small bowl, whisk olive oil, lemon juice, oregano, garlic, salt, and pepper.
3. Place chicken in a baking dish and pour the mixture over it.
4. Toss to coat evenly.
5. Bake for 30 minutes or until the chicken is cooked through and golden.
6. Spoon pan juices over the chicken before serving.

Nutritional value per serving: Calories: 260, Carbs: 1g, Fiber: 0g, Sugars: 0g, Protein: 24g, Saturated fat: 2g, Unsaturated fat: 10g

Difficulty rating: ★☆☆☆☆

Tips for ingredient variations: Add sliced bell peppers or onions to roast alongside. Use boneless chicken if preferred.

Chicken Skillet with Farro and Greens

Number of servings: 2

Preparation time: 10 minutes

Cooking time: 20 minutes

Ingredients:

- 1 tbsp extra virgin olive oil
- 1 small shallot or onion, chopped
- 1 small boneless, skinless chicken breast, diced
- ½ cup cooked farro
- 1 cup baby spinach or arugula
- Juice of ½ lemon
- Salt and pepper to taste

Directions:

1. Heat olive oil in a medium skillet over medium heat.
2. Add shallot and cook for 2 minutes.
3. Cook for 6 to 7 minutes after adding the diced chicken, or until it is no longer pink.
4. Stir in cooked farro and greens. Cook 2–3 minutes until greens are wilted and farro is warmed through.
5. Drizzle with lemon juice and season with salt and pepper.
6. Serve warm.

Nutritional value per serving: Calories: 320, Carbs: 28g, Fiber: 5g, Sugars: 2g, Protein: 25g, Saturated fat: 1g, Unsaturated fat: 8g

Difficulty rating: ★★☆☆☆

Tips for ingredient variations: Swap farro with brown rice or barley. Add a pinch of chili flakes for a little heat.

Baked Chicken Breast with Capers and Parsley

Number of servings: 2

Preparation time: 10 minutes

Cooking time: 20 minutes

Ingredients:

- 2 boneless, skinless chicken breasts
- 1 tbsp extra virgin olive oil
- 1 tbsp lemon juice
- 1 tbsp capers, rinsed
- 2 tbsp chopped fresh parsley
- ¼ tsp salt
- ¼ tsp black pepper

Directions:

1. Preheat oven to 375°F (190°C).
2. Place chicken breasts in a small baking dish.
3. Drizzle with olive oil and lemon juice.
4. Sprinkle with capers, parsley, salt, and pepper.
5. Cover with foil and bake for 15 minutes.
6. Uncover and bake an additional 5 minutes until chicken is cooked through.
7. Spoon pan juices over chicken and serve.

Nutritional value per serving: Calories: 210, Carbs: 1g, Fiber: 0g, Sugars: 0g, Protein: 27g, Saturated fat: 1g, Unsaturated fat: 7g

Difficulty rating: ★☆☆☆☆

Tips for ingredient variations: Add sliced zucchini or cherry tomatoes to the baking dish for a full meal in one pan.

Chicken with Garlic Sautéed Spinach

Number of servings: 2

Preparation time: 10 minutes

Cooking time: 15 minutes

Ingredients:

- 2 small boneless, skinless chicken breasts
- 1 tbsp extra virgin olive oil
- 2 cups fresh spinach, rinsed and trimmed
- 2 garlic cloves, thinly sliced
- ½ tsp salt
- ¼ tsp black pepper
- 1 tbsp lemon juice (optional)

Directions:

1. Pat chicken breasts dry and season both sides with salt and pepper.
2. In a large skillet, heat ½ tablespoon of olive oil over medium heat.
3. Add the chicken and cook for 5–6 minutes per side, or until fully cooked through and golden brown. Remove from skillet and cover loosely to keep warm.
4. In the same skillet, heat the remaining ½ tablespoon of olive oil.
5. Add sliced garlic and sauté for 30 seconds until fragrant.
6. Add spinach and cook for 2–3 minutes, stirring, until wilted.
7. Add a splash of lemon juice if using, and stir.
8. Serve the chicken alongside the spinach.

Nutritional value per serving: Calories: 280, Carbs: 3g, Fiber: 1g, Sugars: 0g, Protein: 34g, Saturated fat: 2g, Unsaturated fat: 10g

Difficulty rating: ★★☆☆☆

Tips for ingredient variations: Use baby kale or Swiss chard instead of spinach. Add a pinch of chili flakes for extra flavor.

Chicken Roll-Ups with Feta, Spinach, and Herbs

Number of servings: 2

Preparation time: 15 minutes

Cooking time: 20 minutes

Ingredients:

- 2 thin chicken cutlets (or pound chicken breasts to flatten)
- 1 tbsp extra virgin olive oil
- ½ cup fresh spinach, chopped
- 2 tbsp crumbled feta cheese
- 1 tbsp chopped fresh parsley or dill
- ¼ tsp garlic powder
- ½ tsp salt
- ¼ tsp black pepper

Directions:

1. Preheat oven to 375°F (190°C).
2. In a bowl, combine chopped spinach, feta, parsley (or dill), garlic powder, and a pinch of salt and pepper.
3. Lay the chicken cutlets flat. Spoon the filling mixture onto each and roll tightly. Secure with toothpicks if needed.
4. Place roll-ups in a small baking dish. Drizzle with olive oil and sprinkle with remaining salt and pepper.
5. The chicken should be cooked through and have a hint of golden color after 18 to 20 minutes in the oven.
6. Let rest for 5 minutes before serving.

Nutritional value per serving: Calories: 300, Carbs: 2g, Fiber: 0g, Sugars: 0g, Protein: 36g, Saturated fat: 3g, Unsaturated fat: 11g

Difficulty rating: ★★☆☆☆

Tips for ingredient variations: Try with goat cheese instead of feta, or add finely chopped sun-dried tomatoes to the filling.

Special Mains – Unique, meat-free or poultry/fish dishes

Turkey meatballs (lean) in herbed tomato sauce

Number of servings: 4

Preparation time: 15 minutes

Cooking time: 20 minutes

Ingredients:

- 1 lb lean ground turkey (93% lean or higher)
- ¼ cup whole wheat breadcrumbs
- 1 egg
- 1 garlic clove, minced
- 1 tbsp chopped fresh parsley
- ½ tsp dried oregano
- ¼ tsp salt
- 2 tbsp extra virgin olive oil
- 2 cups low-sodium crushed tomatoes
- ½ tsp dried basil
- ¼ tsp black pepper

Directions:

1. In a bowl, mix turkey, breadcrumbs, egg, garlic, parsley, oregano, and salt.
2. Form into small meatballs, about 1 inch in diameter.
3. Heat olive oil in a large skillet over medium heat. Add meatballs and brown for 5–6 minutes, turning occasionally.
4. Add crushed tomatoes, basil, and black pepper to the pan.
5. Reduce heat to low, cover, and simmer for 10–12 minutes until meatballs are cooked through.
6. Serve warm.

Nutritional value per serving: Calories: 280, Carbs: 9g, Fiber: 2g, Sugars: 4g, Protein: 27g, Saturated fat: 2g, Unsaturated fat: 10g

Difficulty rating: ★★☆☆☆

Tips for ingredient variations: Swap parsley with fresh basil. Serve over brown rice, quinoa, or with a side of sautéed greens.

Grilled vegetable skewers with halloumi

Number of servings: 2

Preparation time: 10 minutes

Cooking time: 10 minutes

Ingredients:

- 1 small zucchini, sliced
- 1 red bell pepper, cut into chunks
- 1 red onion, cut into wedges
- ½ cup cherry tomatoes
- 4 oz halloumi cheese, cut into cubes
- 1 tbsp extra virgin olive oil
- ½ tsp dried oregano
- Pinch of black pepper

Directions:

1. Preheat grill or grill pan to medium heat.
2. Thread vegetables and halloumi onto skewers, alternating pieces.
3. Brush with olive oil and sprinkle with oregano and black pepper.
4. Grill for 8–10 minutes, turning occasionally, until veggies are tender and halloumi is golden.
5. Serve hot or at room temperature.

Nutritional value per serving: Calories: 290, Carbs: 11g, Fiber: 3g, Sugars: 6g, Protein: 14g, Saturated fat: 7g, Unsaturated fat: 9g

Difficulty rating: ★★☆☆☆

Tips for ingredient variations: Add mushrooms or eggplant. Use feta instead of halloumi, added after grilling.

Chickpea and vegetable stuffed eggplant

Number of servings: 2
Preparation time: 15 minutes
Cooking time: 25 minutes

Ingredients:

- 1 medium eggplant, halved lengthwise
- 1 tbsp extra virgin olive oil
- ½ cup canned chickpeas, rinsed and drained
- ¼ cup diced zucchini
- ¼ cup chopped tomatoes
- 1 garlic clove, minced
- 1 tbsp chopped parsley
- ¼ tsp salt
- ¼ tsp black pepper
- 1 tbsp crumbled feta (optional)

Directions:

1. Preheat oven to 375°F (190°C).
2. Scoop out some of the eggplant flesh, leaving a shell about ½ inch thick. Chop the scooped flesh.
3. Heat olive oil in a pan over medium heat. Sauté garlic, chopped eggplant, zucchini, and tomatoes for 5–6 minutes.
4. Stir in chickpeas, parsley, salt, and pepper. Cook for 2 more minutes.
5. Fill the eggplant halves with the mixture and place on a baking sheet.
6. Bake for 20 minutes until tender. Sprinkle with feta if using.

Nutritional value per serving: Calories: 220, Carbs: 24g, Fiber: 7g, Sugars: 6g, Protein: 6g, Saturated fat: 2g, Unsaturated fat: 8g

Difficulty rating: ★★☆☆☆

Tips for ingredient variations: Add a spoonful of cooked quinoa to the filling for extra protein and texture.

Vegetable lasagna with whole grain pasta and ricotta

Number of servings: 4
Preparation time: 20 minutes
Cooking time: 25 minutes

Ingredients:

- 4 whole wheat lasagna noodles, cooked and drained
- 1 zucchini, sliced thin
- ½ cup baby spinach
- 1 cup low-sodium marinara sauce
- ½ cup ricotta cheese (part-skim)
- ¼ cup grated parmesan cheese
- 1 tbsp extra virgin olive oil
- ½ tsp dried basil
- ¼ tsp black pepper

Directions:

1. Preheat oven to 375°F (190°C).
2. In a skillet, heat olive oil and sauté zucchini for 4–5 minutes until tender.
3. In a small baking dish, spread a spoonful of marinara sauce.
4. Layer noodles, sautéed zucchini, spinach, ricotta, and marinara. Repeat layers.
5. Top with parmesan and dried basil.
6. Cover with foil and bake for 20 minutes. Bake for a further five minutes, or until the top is brown.
7. Let rest for 5 minutes before serving.

Nutritional value per serving: Calories: 290, Carbs: 28g, Fiber: 5g, Sugars: 6g, Protein: 12g, Saturated fat: 4g, Unsaturated fat: 6g

Difficulty rating: ★★★☆☆

Tips for ingredient variations: Add mushrooms or red peppers. Use low-fat cottage cheese instead of ricotta if preferred.

Whole Wheat Pita Pizza with Olives, Veggies, and Herbs

Number of servings: 1
Preparation time: 10 minutes
Cooking time: 10 minutes

Ingredients:

- 1 whole wheat pita bread
- 2 tbsp tomato sauce (no added sugar)
- ¼ cup shredded mozzarella cheese (optional)
- ¼ cup chopped bell pepper
- ¼ cup sliced zucchini or mushrooms
- 4–5 black or green olives, sliced
- ½ tsp dried oregano
- 1 tsp extra virgin olive oil

Directions:

1. Preheat oven to 400°F (200°C).
2. Place the pita on a baking sheet and spread the tomato sauce evenly on top.
3. Add the cheese if using, then top with vegetables and olives.
4. Sprinkle with oregano and drizzle with olive oil.
5. Bake for 8–10 minutes, or until the pita is crisp and the veggies are tender.
6. Serve warm, cut into slices.

Nutritional value per serving: Calories: 280, Carbs: 28g, Fiber: 5g, Sugars: 4g, Protein: 9g, Saturated fat: 2g, Unsaturated fat: 7g

Difficulty rating: ★☆☆☆☆

Tips for ingredient variations: Use fresh basil instead of oregano. Try crumbled feta instead of mozzarella or add a few cherry tomatoes for extra sweetness.

Baked Tofu with Lemon, Garlic, and Olive Oil

Number of servings: 2
Preparation time: 10 minutes
Cooking time: 25 minutes

Ingredients:

- 8 oz firm tofu, drained and cut into cubes
- 1 tbsp extra virgin olive oil
- 1 tbsp lemon juice
- 1 garlic clove, finely chopped
- ½ tsp dried thyme or rosemary
- Pinch of salt
- Pinch of black pepper

Directions:

1. Preheat oven to 375°F (190°C).
2. In a small bowl, mix olive oil, lemon juice, garlic, herbs, salt, and pepper.
3. Gently toss tofu cubes in the mixture to coat evenly.
4. Place tofu on a baking tray lined with parchment paper.
5. Bake for 20–25 minutes, turning once halfway through, until golden and firm.
6. Serve warm with steamed vegetables or a grain.

Nutritional value per serving: Calories: 180, Carbs: 4g, Fiber: 1g, Sugars: 0g, Protein: 12g, Saturated fat: 1g, Unsaturated fat: 8g

Difficulty rating: ★★☆☆☆

Tips for ingredient variations: Add sliced red onion or bell pepper to roast with the tofu. Serve over couscous or quinoa for a complete meal.

Pasta e Fagioli (pasta and beans, no meat broth)

Number of servings: 4
Preparation time: 10 minutes
Cooking time: 20 minutes

Ingredients:

- 1 tbsp extra virgin olive oil
- 1 small onion, chopped
- 1 celery stalk, diced
- 1 carrot, diced
- 1 garlic clove, minced
- 1½ cups canned cannellini or navy beans (rinsed and drained)
- 4 cups low-sodium vegetable broth
- ½ cup small whole wheat pasta (like ditalini or elbows)
- ¼ tsp dried thyme
- ¼ tsp salt
- Black pepper to taste
- Fresh parsley (optional)

Directions:

1. Heat olive oil in a medium pot over medium heat.
2. Add onion, celery, and carrot. Cook for 5–7 minutes until softened.
3. Stir in garlic and thyme. Cook 1 minute more.
4. Add beans and vegetable broth. Bring to a boil.
5. Add pasta and reduce heat. Simmer for 10 minutes, or until pasta is tender.
6. Season with salt and pepper.
7. Serve warm, topped with fresh parsley if desired.

Nutritional value per serving: Calories: 240, Carbs: 32g, Fiber: 7g, Sugars: 4g, Protein: 9g, Saturated fat: 1g, Unsaturated fat: 7g

Difficulty rating: ★★☆☆☆

Tips for ingredient variations: Use lentils instead of beans for a different texture. Add chopped spinach at the end for more greens.

Creamy Polenta with Sautéed Mushrooms

Number of servings: 2

Preparation time: 5 minutes

Cooking time: 15 minutes

Ingredients:

- ½ cup quick-cooking polenta
- 2 cups water
- 1 tbsp extra virgin olive oil
- 1½ cups sliced mushrooms (any variety)
- 1 garlic clove, minced
- 1 tbsp grated Parmesan (optional)
- Pinch of salt
- Pinch of black pepper

Directions:

1. In a medium pot, bring water to a boil. Slowly whisk in the polenta.
2. Reduce heat and cook, stirring often, for 5–7 minutes until creamy.
3. Meanwhile, heat olive oil in a pan over medium heat.
4. Add mushrooms and garlic. Cook for 5–7 minutes until mushrooms are soft and browned.
5. Season both polenta and mushrooms with salt and pepper.
6. Spoon polenta into bowls, top with mushrooms, and add Parmesan if using.

Nutritional value per serving: Calories: 210, Carbs: 23g, Fiber: 3g, Sugars: 1g, Protein: 6g, Saturated fat: 1g, Unsaturated fat: 7g

Difficulty rating: ★★☆☆☆

Tips for ingredient variations: Add chopped fresh herbs like parsley or thyme. Use low-sodium vegetable broth instead of water for added flavor.

Lentil and Eggplant Moussaka (No Red Meat)

Number of servings: 4

Preparation time: 20 minutes

Cooking time: 30 minutes

Ingredients:

- 1 medium eggplant, sliced into ¼-inch rounds
- 1 tbsp extra virgin olive oil
- 1 cup cooked green or brown lentils
- 1 cup low-sodium crushed tomatoes
- 1 small onion, chopped
- 1 garlic clove, minced
- ½ tsp dried oregano
- ¼ tsp cinnamon (optional)
- Pinch of salt and black pepper
- ½ cup plain Greek yogurt
- 1 egg
- 2 tbsp grated Parmesan (optional)

Directions:

1. Preheat oven to 375°F (190°C).
2. Brush eggplant slices lightly with olive oil. Roast on a baking sheet for 15–20 minutes until soft.
3. In a skillet, sauté onion and garlic for 3–4 minutes. Add lentils, tomatoes, oregano, cinnamon, salt, and pepper. Simmer for 10 minutes.
4. In a bowl, mix yogurt with the egg and Parmesan (if using).
5. In a small baking dish, layer half the eggplant, then the lentil mixture, then the rest of the eggplant.
6. Pour yogurt mixture on top and spread evenly.

1. Bake for 20–25 minutes until golden and set. Let cool slightly before serving.

Nutritional value per serving: Calories: 270, Carbs: 26g, Fiber: 8g, Sugars: 6g, Protein: 13g, Saturated fat: 2g, Unsaturated fat: 9g

Difficulty rating: ★★★☆☆

Tips for ingredient variations: Use zucchini slices instead of eggplant. Add chopped parsley for a fresh finish.

Zucchini Fritters with Yogurt Sauce

Number of servings: 4

Preparation time: 15 minutes

Cooking time: 10 minutes

Ingredients:

- 2 medium zucchinis, grated
- ¼ tsp salt
- ¼ cup chopped green onion
- ¼ cup crumbled feta (optional)
- 1 egg
- ¼ cup whole wheat flour
- 1 tbsp chopped fresh mint or parsley
- 1 tbsp extra virgin olive oil (for cooking)

Yogurt Sauce:

- ½ cup plain Greek yogurt
- 1 tbsp lemon juice
- 1 tbsp chopped dill or mint

Directions:

1. Squeeze off extra water from the grated zucchini using a fresh paper towel or kitchen towel.
2. In a bowl, combine zucchini, green onion, egg, flour, herbs, and feta (if using). Mix well.
3. Heat olive oil in a skillet over medium heat.
4. Scoop spoonfuls of the mixture into the skillet, flattening slightly. Cook 3–4 minutes per side until golden.
5. In a small bowl, mix yogurt, lemon juice, and herbs for the sauce.
6. Serve fritters warm with a dollop of yogurt sauce on the side.

Nutritional value per serving: Calories: 180, Carbs: 10g, Fiber: 2g, Sugars: 3g, Protein: 8g, Saturated fat: 2g, Unsaturated fat: 6g

Difficulty rating: ★★☆☆☆

Tips for ingredient variations: Use grated carrots or sweet potato in place of some zucchini. For dairy-free, skip the feta and use a plant-based yogurt for the sauce.

Brown Rice and Vegetable Stuffed Grape Leaves

Number of servings: 4 (makes about 16 rolls)

Preparation time: 20 minutes

Cooking time: 20 minutes

Ingredients:

- 16 jarred grape leaves (rinsed and drained)
- 1 cup cooked brown rice
- ½ cup diced cucumber
- ¼ cup finely chopped tomato
- 2 tbsp chopped parsley
- 2 tbsp chopped mint
- 2 tbsp lemon juice
- 1 tbsp extra virgin olive oil
- ¼ tsp salt

Directions:

1. Lay grape leaves flat on a clean surface, shiny side down.
2. In a bowl, combine rice, cucumber, tomato, herbs, lemon juice, olive oil, and salt. Mix well.
3. Place 1 tablespoon of filling near the base of each grape leaf. Fold in sides and roll tightly.
4. Arrange rolls seam-side down in a shallow pan. Add a splash of water, cover, and steam on low heat for 15–20 minutes.
5. Let cool slightly before serving.

Nutritional value per serving: Calories: 160, Carbs: 24g, Fiber: 3g, Sugars: 2g, Protein: 3g, Saturated fat: 0g, Unsaturated fat: 5g

Difficulty rating: ★★☆☆☆

Tips for ingredient variations: Add a spoonful of cooked lentils or chickpeas to the filling for extra protein.

Falafel Baked in the Oven with Tahini

Number of servings: 4 (makes 12 falafel)

Preparation time: 15 minutes

Cooking time: 25 minutes

Ingredients:

- One can (15 oz) of rinsed and drained chickpeas
- ¼ cup chopped parsley
- ¼ cup chopped onion
- 1 garlic clove, minced
- 1 tsp ground cumin
- 1 tsp ground coriander
- 2 tbsp whole wheat flour
- 1 tbsp extra virgin olive oil (for brushing)

Tahini Sauce:

- 2 tbsp tahini
- 2 tbsp water
- 1 tbsp lemon juice
- Pinch of salt

Directions:

1. Preheat oven to 400°F (200°C). Line a baking sheet with parchment paper.
2. In a food processor, blend chickpeas, parsley, onion, garlic, spices, and flour until chunky but sticky.
3. Form mixture into small balls or patties. Place on the baking sheet.
4. Brush tops lightly with olive oil.
5. Bake for 25 minutes, flipping halfway through, until golden.
6. In a small bowl, whisk tahini, water, lemon juice, and salt until smooth.
7. Serve falafel warm with tahini sauce on the side.

Nutritional value per serving: Calories: 220, Carbs: 22g, Fiber: 6g, Sugars: 1g, Protein: 8g, Saturated fat: 1g, Unsaturated fat: 10g

Difficulty rating: ★★☆☆☆

Tips for ingredient variations: Add spinach or grated carrot to the mixture for color and extra nutrients.

Gnocchi with Cherry Tomatoes and Basil

Number of servings: 2

Preparation time: 5 minutes

Cooking time: 10 minutes

Ingredients:

- 1 cup whole wheat gnocchi
- 1 cup cherry tomatoes, halved
- 1 tbsp extra virgin olive oil
- 1 clove garlic, minced
- ¼ tsp salt
- ¼ cup chopped fresh basil
- 1 tbsp grated parmesan (optional)

Directions:

1. Bring a pot of water to a boil. Add gnocchi and cook according to package instructions (usually 2–3 minutes). Drain and set aside.
2. In a skillet, heat olive oil over medium heat. Add garlic and sauté for 1 minute.
3. Add cherry tomatoes and cook for 4–5 minutes, until soft and slightly blistered.
4. Add cooked gnocchi and salt. Toss gently to combine and heat through.
5. Stir in fresh basil just before serving.
6. Sprinkle with parmesan if desired and serve warm.

Nutritional value per serving: Calories: 260, Carbs: 36g, Fiber: 4g, Sugars: 4g, Protein: 7g, Saturated fat: 1g, Unsaturated fat: 7g

Difficulty rating: ★★☆☆☆

Tips for ingredient variations: Add a handful of spinach or arugula for more greens. Use store-bought gnocchi made with sweet potato or cauliflower for variety.

Shakshuka (eggs cooked in tomato and pepper sauce)

Number of servings: 2

Preparation time: 10 minutes

Cooking time: 15 minutes

Ingredients:

- 1 tbsp extra virgin olive oil
- 1 small onion, chopped
- 1 small red bell pepper, diced
- 1 garlic clove, minced
- 1 cup canned crushed tomatoes (no salt added)
- ¼ tsp ground cumin
- ¼ tsp smoked paprika (optional)
- 2 large eggs
- Pinch of salt
- Pinch of black pepper
- Fresh parsley or cilantro, chopped (optional)

Directions:

1. Heat olive oil in a medium non-stick skillet over medium heat.
2. Add onion and bell pepper, and sauté for 5–6 minutes until softened.
3. Stir in garlic, cumin, and paprika. Cook for 1 minute.
4. Pour in crushed tomatoes. Simmer uncovered for 5 minutes, stirring occasionally.
5. Gently crack the eggs into the sauce after creating two little wells.
6. Cover the skillet and cook for 4–5 minutes, or until egg whites are set but yolks remain soft.
7. Season with salt and pepper, and garnish with chopped herbs if desired. Serve warm.

Nutritional value per serving: Calories: 180, Carbs: 10g, Fiber: 3g, Sugars: 5g, Protein: 9g, Saturated fat: 2g, Unsaturated fat: 8g

Difficulty rating: ★★☆☆☆

Tips for ingredient variations: Add chopped zucchini or spinach for more veggies. Use only egg whites if lowering cholesterol.

Cauliflower Steaks with Yogurt and Za'atar

Number of servings: 2

Preparation time: 10 minutes

Cooking time: 20 minutes

Ingredients:

- 1 medium head cauliflower
- 2 tbsp extra virgin olive oil
- ½ tsp salt
- ½ tsp black pepper
- ½ cup plain Greek yogurt
- ½ tsp za'atar seasoning
- 1 tsp lemon juice

Directions:

1. Preheat oven to 425°F (220°C).
2. Remove outer leaves from cauliflower and trim the stem. Slice into ¾-inch "steaks" from the center.
3. Place on a baking sheet lined with parchment paper. Brush both sides with olive oil and sprinkle with salt and pepper.
4. Roast for 20 minutes, flipping halfway through, until golden and tender.
5. Meanwhile, mix Greek yogurt, za'atar, and lemon juice in a small bowl.
6. Serve cauliflower steaks warm with a dollop of yogurt sauce on top or on the side.

Nutritional value per serving: Calories: 160, Carbs: 11g, Fiber: 4g, Sugars: 4g, Protein: 6g, Saturated fat: 2g, Unsaturated fat: 9g

Difficulty rating: ★★☆☆☆

Tips for ingredient variations: If you don't have za'atar, use a mix of thyme, sesame seeds, and sumac or a dash of oregano.

Sides – Easy, flavorful additions

Roasted Carrots with Olive Oil and Thyme

Number of servings: 4

Preparation time: 10 minutes

Cooking time: 25 minutes

Ingredients:

- 1 lb (about 6 medium) carrots, peeled and cut into sticks
- 1½ tbsp extra virgin olive oil
- ½ tsp dried thyme (or 1 tsp fresh thyme)
- ¼ tsp salt
- ¼ tsp black pepper

Directions:

1. Preheat oven to 400°F (200°C).
2. Place the carrot sticks on a baking sheet.
3. Drizzle with olive oil and sprinkle with thyme, salt, and pepper.
4. Toss to coat evenly and spread into a single layer.
5. Roast for 20–25 minutes, flipping halfway, until tender and lightly browned.
6. Serve warm or at room temperature.

Nutritional value per serving: Calories: 90, Carbs: 11g, Fiber: 3g, Sugars: 5g, Protein: 1g, Saturated fat: 0g, Unsaturated fat: 6g

Difficulty rating: ★☆☆☆☆

Tips for ingredient variations: Add a squeeze of lemon juice before serving for extra brightness. Try with rosemary or cumin instead of thyme.

Cucumber Yogurt Salad with Mint

Number of servings: 2

Preparation time: 10 minutes

Cooking time: 0 minutes

Ingredients:

- 1 cup plain Greek yogurt
- 1 medium cucumber, peeled and diced
- 1 tbsp fresh mint, chopped (or ½ tsp dried mint)
- ½ small garlic clove, minced (optional)
- ½ tbsp extra virgin olive oil
- Pinch of salt

Directions:

1. In a medium bowl, combine yogurt, diced cucumber, mint, garlic (if using), and salt.
2. Stir well until smooth and evenly mixed.
3. Drizzle with olive oil before serving.
4. Serve chilled or at room temperature.

Nutritional value per serving: Calories: 100, Carbs: 6g, Fiber: 1g, Sugars: 4g, Protein: 9g, Saturated fat: 2g, Unsaturated fat: 4g

Difficulty rating: ★☆☆☆☆

Tips for ingredient variations: Add a squeeze of lemon juice for extra tang. Swap mint with dill for a different twist.

Steamed Broccoli with Lemon Drizzle

Number of servings: 2

Preparation time: 5 minutes

Cooking time: 8 minutes

Ingredients:

- 2 cups broccoli florets
- 1 tbsp extra virgin olive oil
- 1 tbsp fresh lemon juice
- Pinch of salt
- Pinch of black pepper

Directions:

1. Steam broccoli in a steamer basket or pot with 1 inch of water for 6–8 minutes, until tender but bright green.
2. Drain well and transfer to a serving bowl.
3. Drizzle with olive oil and lemon juice.
4. Sprinkle with salt and pepper.
5. Serve warm or slightly cooled.

Nutritional value per serving: Calories: 100, Carbs: 7g, Fiber: 3g, Sugars: 2g, Protein: 3g, Saturated fat: 1g, Unsaturated fat: 7g

Difficulty rating: ★☆☆☆☆

Tips for ingredient variations: Add chopped garlic or lemon zest for extra flavor. Use frozen broccoli if fresh is not available.

Simple Greek Salad with Feta and Olives

Number of servings: 2

Preparation time: 10 minutes

Cooking time: 0 minutes

Ingredients:

- 1 cup cherry tomatoes, halved
- 1 small cucumber, diced
- ¼ red onion, thinly sliced
- ¼ cup kalamata olives, pitted and halved
- ¼ cup crumbled feta cheese
- 1 tbsp extra virgin olive oil
- ½ tbsp red wine vinegar or lemon juice
- Pinch of dried oregano
- Pinch of black pepper

Directions:

1. In a large bowl, combine tomatoes, cucumber, red onion, and olives.
2. Add feta cheese on top.
3. Drizzle with olive oil and vinegar (or lemon juice).
4. Sprinkle with oregano and black pepper.
5. Toss gently and serve immediately.

Nutritional value per serving: Calories: 180, Carbs: 8g, Fiber: 2g, Sugars: 4g, Protein: 5g, Saturated fat: 3g, Unsaturated fat: 10g

Difficulty rating: ★☆☆☆☆

Tips for ingredient variations: Add sliced green pepper for crunch. Replace feta with a few avocado cubes for a dairy-free version.

Roasted Peppers with Garlic and Olive Oil

Number of servings: 4

Preparation time: 10 minutes

Cooking time: 20 minutes

Ingredients:

- 3 bell peppers (red, yellow, or orange), sliced into strips
- 2 garlic cloves, thinly sliced
- 2 tbsp extra virgin olive oil
- ¼ tsp salt
- ¼ tsp black pepper

Directions:

1. Preheat the oven to 400°F (200°C).
2. Place sliced peppers and garlic on a baking sheet.
3. Drizzle with olive oil and toss to coat evenly.
4. Sprinkle with salt and pepper.
5. Roast for 20 minutes, stirring once halfway, until peppers are tender and slightly caramelized.
6. Serve warm or at room temperature.

Nutritional value per serving: Calories: 110, Carbs: 9g, Fiber: 3g, Sugars: 6g, Protein: 1g, Saturated fat: 1g, Unsaturated fat: 7g

Difficulty rating: ★☆☆☆☆

Tips for ingredient variations: Add a splash of balsamic vinegar before serving. Use a mix of colored peppers for extra visual appeal and nutrition.

Sautéed Greens with Lemon

Number of servings: 2

Preparation time: 5 minutes

Cooking time: 7 minutes

Ingredients:

- 4 cups fresh spinach or kale, chopped
- 1 tbsp extra virgin olive oil
- 1 garlic clove, minced
- 1 tbsp lemon juice
- Pinch of salt
- Pinch of black pepper

Directions:

1. Heat olive oil in a large skillet over medium heat.
2. Add garlic and cook for 30 seconds until fragrant, but not browned.
3. Add greens and sauté for 4–5 minutes until wilted and tender.
4. Drizzle with lemon juice and season with salt and pepper.
5. Serve warm.

Nutritional value per serving: Calories: 90, Carbs: 4g, Fiber: 2g, Sugars: 1g, Protein: 2g, Saturated fat: 1g, Unsaturated fat: 6g

Difficulty rating: ★☆☆☆☆

Tips for ingredient variations: Try Swiss chard or mustard greens. Add crushed red pepper flakes if you enjoy a little heat.

Tomato and Red Onion Salad

Number of servings: 2

Preparation time: 10 minutes

Cooking time: 0 minutes

Ingredients:

- 2 medium tomatoes, sliced
- ¼ small red onion, thinly sliced
- 1 tbsp extra virgin olive oil
- 1 tsp red wine vinegar or lemon juice
- Pinch of salt
- Pinch of black pepper
- Optional: 1 tsp chopped fresh oregano or parsley

Directions:

1. In a bowl, combine sliced tomatoes and red onion.
2. Drizzle with olive oil and vinegar (or lemon juice).
3. Sprinkle with salt, pepper, and herbs if using.
4. Toss gently and let sit for 5 minutes before serving.

Nutritional value per serving: Calories: 80, Carbs: 7g, Fiber: 2g, Sugars: 5g, Protein: 1g, Saturated fat: 0g, Unsaturated fat: 6g

Difficulty rating: ★☆☆☆☆

Tips for ingredient variations: Add sliced cucumber or a few crumbled olives for extra flavor. Use heirloom tomatoes when in season for color and taste.

Quinoa with Parsley and Olive Oil

Number of servings: 4

Preparation time: 5 minutes

Cooking time: 15 minutes

Ingredients:

- 1 cup dry quinoa
- 2 cups water
- 2 tbsp chopped fresh parsley
- 2 tbsp extra virgin olive oil
- ¼ tsp salt
- Optional: 1 tbsp lemon juice

Directions:

1. Rinse quinoa under cold water.
2. In a medium saucepan, bring water and salt to a boil.
3. Reduce the heat, add the quinoa, cover, and simmer for 12 to 15 minutes, until the water has been absorbed.
4. Remove from heat and let sit covered for 5 minutes.
5. Fluff with a fork, then stir in parsley, olive oil, and lemon juice if using.
6. Serve warm or at room temperature.

Nutritional value per serving: Calories: 180, Carbs: 24g, Fiber: 3g, Sugars: 1g, Protein: 5g, Saturated fat: 0g, Unsaturated fat: 7g

Difficulty rating: ★☆☆☆☆

Tips for ingredient variations: Add chopped mint or scallions. Mix in a handful of diced cucumber or cherry tomatoes for a quick salad version.

Roasted Zucchini with Oregano

Number of servings: 2

Preparation time: 5 minutes

Cooking time: 20 minutes

Ingredients:

- 2 medium zucchinis, sliced into half-moons
- 1 tbsp extra virgin olive oil
- ½ tsp dried oregano
- ¼ tsp salt
- ¼ tsp black pepper

Directions:

1. Preheat the oven to 400°F (200°C).
2. Place zucchini slices on a baking sheet lined with parchment paper.
3. Drizzle with olive oil and sprinkle with oregano, salt, and pepper.
4. Toss gently to coat.
5. Roast for 18–20 minutes, or until tender and lightly golden.
6. Serve warm or at room temperature.

Nutritional value per serving: Calories: 90, Carbs: 6g, Fiber: 2g, Sugars: 4g, Protein: 1g, Saturated fat: 1g, Unsaturated fat: 6g

Difficulty rating: ★☆☆☆☆

Tips for ingredient variations: Add sliced red onion or crushed garlic before roasting. Swap oregano for thyme or rosemary for a flavor twist.

Beet and Orange Salad

Number of servings: 2

Preparation time: 10 minutes

Cooking time: 0 minutes (using pre-cooked beets)

Ingredients:

- 2 medium cooked beets, peeled and sliced
- 1 medium orange, peeled and sliced into rounds
- 1 tbsp extra virgin olive oil
- ½ tsp red wine vinegar or lemon juice
- Pinch of salt
- Pinch of black pepper
- Optional: 1 tsp chopped fresh parsley

Directions:

1. Arrange beet and orange slices on a plate, alternating them.
2. In a small bowl, mix olive oil, vinegar or lemon juice, salt, and pepper.
3. Drizzle dressing over the salad.
4. Sprinkle with parsley if using, and serve chilled or at room temperature.

Nutritional value per serving: Calories: 110, Carbs: 16g, Fiber: 3g, Sugars: 11g, Protein: 2g, Saturated fat: 0g, Unsaturated fat: 7g

Difficulty rating: ★☆☆☆☆

Tips for ingredient variations: Use pre-cooked vacuum-sealed beets for convenience. Add a few walnut pieces for texture and healthy fats.

Cabbage Salad with Olive Oil and Vinegar

Number of servings: 2
Preparation time: 10 minutes
Cooking time: 0 minutes

Ingredients:

- 2 cups shredded green cabbage
- ¼ cup shredded carrot (optional)
- 1 tbsp extra virgin olive oil
- 1 tbsp apple cider vinegar or red wine vinegar
- ¼ tsp salt
- ¼ tsp black pepper

Directions:

1. In a large bowl, combine shredded cabbage and carrot (if using).
2. Drizzle with olive oil and vinegar.
3. Add salt and pepper.
4. Toss well to coat evenly.
5. Let sit for 5–10 minutes before serving to soften slightly.

Nutritional value per serving: Calories: 80, Carbs: 7g, Fiber: 2g, Sugars: 3g, Protein: 1g, Saturated fat: 1g, Unsaturated fat: 6g

Difficulty rating: ★☆☆☆☆

Tips for ingredient variations: Add a squeeze of lemon or a pinch of cumin. For a more tender salad, massage the cabbage with your hands after adding the dressing.

Roasted Sweet Potato Wedges

Number of servings: 2
Preparation time: 5 minutes
Cooking time: 25 minutes

Ingredients:

- 1 large sweet potato, scrubbed and cut into wedges
- 1 tbsp extra virgin olive oil
- ½ tsp paprika
- ¼ tsp salt
- ¼ tsp black pepper

Directions:

1. Preheat the oven to 425°F (220°C).
2. Place sweet potato wedges on a baking sheet.
3. Drizzle with olive oil and sprinkle with paprika, salt, and pepper.
4. Toss to coat evenly.
5. Roast for 20–25 minutes, turning once halfway through, until golden and tender.
6. Serve warm.

Nutritional value per serving: Calories: 140, Carbs: 22g, Fiber: 4g, Sugars: 5g, Protein: 2g, Saturated fat: 1g, Unsaturated fat: 8g

Difficulty rating: ★☆☆☆☆

Tips for ingredient variations: Use smoked paprika or a dash of cinnamon for a flavor change. Serve with a side of plain yogurt for dipping.

Lentil Salad with Lemon Dressing

Number of servings: 4

Preparation time: 10 minutes

Cooking time: 20 minutes

Ingredients:

- 1 cup dry green or brown lentils
- 3 cups water
- ½ cup diced cucumber
- ½ cup cherry tomatoes, halved
- ¼ cup chopped red onion
- 2 tbsp chopped parsley
- 2 tbsp extra virgin olive oil
- 1 tbsp fresh lemon juice
- ½ tsp salt
- ¼ tsp black pepper

Directions:

1. Rinse the lentils under cold water.
2. In a medium pot, bring water to a boil. Add lentils, reduce heat, and simmer for 15–20 minutes until tender. Drain and let cool slightly.
3. Lentils, cucumber, cherry tomatoes, red onion, and parsley should all be combined in a big bowl.
4. Drizzle with olive oil and lemon juice.
5. Add salt and pepper, then toss gently to combine.
6. Serve chilled or at room temperature.

Nutritional value per serving: Calories: 210, Carbs: 28g, Fiber: 9g, Sugars: 3g, Protein: 10g, Saturated fat: 1g, Unsaturated fat: 6g

Difficulty rating: ★★☆☆☆

Tips for ingredient variations: Add diced bell pepper or crumble a small amount of feta for extra flavor.

Marinated Mushrooms with Herbs

Number of servings: 4

Preparation time: 10 minutes

Cooking time: 10 minutes

Ingredients:

- 2 cups button or cremini mushrooms, sliced
- 2 tbsp extra virgin olive oil
- 1 tbsp red wine vinegar
- 1 clove garlic, minced
- 1 tbsp chopped fresh parsley
- ½ tsp dried oregano
- ¼ tsp salt
- ¼ tsp black pepper

Directions:

1. In a skillet, heat 1 tablespoon of olive oil over medium heat.
2. Add mushrooms and sauté for 5–6 minutes until softened and lightly browned.
3. Transfer mushrooms to a bowl.
4. Add remaining olive oil, vinegar, garlic, parsley, oregano, salt, and pepper.
5. Toss gently and let marinate for at least 10 minutes before serving.
6. Serve warm or chilled.

Nutritional value per serving: Calories: 120, Carbs: 4g, Fiber: 1g, Sugars: 1g, Protein: 2g, Saturated fat: 1g, Unsaturated fat: 10g

Difficulty rating: ★★☆☆☆

Tips for ingredient variations: Add a few sliced olives or a splash of lemon juice for brightness.

Chickpea Mash with Olive Oil

Number of servings: 2
Preparation time: 5 minutes
Cooking time: 0 minutes

Ingredients:

- 1 cup canned chickpeas, rinsed and drained
- 1 tbsp extra virgin olive oil
- 1 tbsp lemon juice
- ½ tsp ground cumin (optional)
- ¼ tsp salt
- 2 tbsp water (as needed for texture)

Directions:

1. Place chickpeas in a medium bowl.
2. Add olive oil, lemon juice, cumin (if using), and salt.
3. Mash with a fork or potato masher until mostly smooth, adding water 1 tablespoon at a time if too thick.
4. Adjust seasoning to taste.
5. Serve as a dip or spread.

Nutritional value per serving: Calories: 180, Carbs: 18g, Fiber: 5g, Sugars: 2g, Protein: 6g, Saturated fat: 1g, Unsaturated fat: 7g

Difficulty rating: ★☆☆☆☆

Tips for ingredient variations: Mix in chopped herbs or crushed garlic for more flavor. Serve with raw veggies or whole grain toast.

Olive Tapenade with Whole Grain Crackers

Number of servings: 6 (as an appetizer)
Preparation time: 10 minutes
Cooking time: 0 minutes

Ingredients:

- 1 cup pitted black or Kalamata olives
- 1 tbsp capers (rinsed if salted)
- 1 clove garlic
- 1 tbsp fresh lemon juice
- 2 tbsp extra virgin olive oil
- ½ tsp dried thyme or oregano

Directions:

1. Place olives, capers, garlic, and lemon juice in a food processor or blender.
2. Pulse a few times until roughly chopped.
3. Add olive oil and thyme, then pulse again until the mixture forms a coarse paste.
4. Serve with whole grain crackers or as a spread on toast.

Nutritional value per serving: Calories: 100, Carbs: 2g, Fiber: 1g, Sugars: 0g, Protein: 1g, Saturated fat: 1g, Unsaturated fat: 8g

Difficulty rating: ★☆☆☆☆

Tips for ingredient variations: Add a few chopped sun-dried tomatoes or fresh basil for a richer flavor.

Blanched Green Beans with Slivered Almonds

Number of servings: 4
Preparation time: 5 minutes
Cooking time: 7 minutes

Ingredients:

- 1 lb fresh green beans, trimmed
- 2 tbsp slivered almonds
- 1 tbsp extra virgin olive oil
- ½ tsp salt
- ¼ tsp black pepper

Directions:

1. Bring a large pot of water to a boil.
2. Add the green beans and cook for 4–5 minutes, until just tender but still bright green.
3. Drain and move right away to a dish of ice water to halt the cooking process. Empty once more.
4. In a dry skillet over medium heat, toast the almonds for 2–3 minutes, stirring constantly, until lightly golden.
5. Toss the green beans with olive oil, salt, and pepper. Sprinkle with toasted almonds and serve.

Nutritional value per serving: Calories: 110, Carbs: 7g, Fiber: 3g, Sugars: 2g, Protein: 3g, Saturated fat: 0g, Unsaturated fat: 7g

Difficulty rating: ★☆☆☆☆

Tips for ingredient variations: Add a squeeze of lemon juice for brightness. Use chopped walnuts or sunflower seeds if preferred.

Grilled Eggplant Rounds with Olive Oil

Number of servings: 2
Preparation time: 5 minutes
Cooking time: 10 minutes

Ingredients:

- 1 medium eggplant, sliced into ½-inch rounds
- 2 tbsp extra virgin olive oil
- ½ tsp salt
- ¼ tsp black pepper
- ½ tsp dried oregano (optional)

Directions:

1. Preheat a grill or grill pan over medium heat.
2. Brush both sides of the eggplant rounds with olive oil and sprinkle with salt, pepper, and oregano (if using).
3. Place eggplant on the grill and cook for 4–5 minutes per side, until golden and tender.
4. Serve warm or at room temperature.

Nutritional value per serving: Calories: 130, Carbs: 9g, Fiber: 4g, Sugars: 5g, Protein: 2g, Saturated fat: 1g, Unsaturated fat: 10g

Difficulty rating: ★☆☆☆☆

Tips for ingredient variations: Add chopped fresh parsley or a touch of balsamic vinegar before serving for extra flavor.

Couscous with Lemon and Mint

Number of servings: 4
Preparation time: 5 minutes
Cooking time: 5 minutes

Ingredients:

- 1 cup whole wheat couscous
- 1 cup boiling water
- 1 tbsp extra virgin olive oil
- 1 tbsp fresh lemon juice
- 2 tbsp chopped fresh mint
- ½ tsp salt

Directions:

1. Place couscous in a large heat-safe bowl.
2. Pour boiling water over it, cover, and let sit for 5 minutes.
3. Fluff with a fork, then stir in olive oil, lemon juice, mint, and salt.
4. Serve warm or chilled.

Nutritional value per serving: Calories: 160, Carbs: 26g, Fiber: 3g, Sugars: 1g, Protein: 5g, Saturated fat: 0g, Unsaturated fat: 5g

Difficulty rating: ★☆☆☆☆

Tips for ingredient variations: Add chopped cucumber or tomato for extra texture. Use parsley instead of mint for a more traditional tabbouleh-like twist.

Tomato, Cucumber, and Parsley Bowl

Number of servings: 2
Preparation time: 10 minutes
Cooking time: 0 minutes

Ingredients:

- 1 large tomato, diced
- 1 medium cucumber, diced
- 2 tbsp chopped fresh parsley
- 1 tbsp extra virgin olive oil
- 1 tsp fresh lemon juice
- ¼ tsp salt
- Pinch of black pepper

Directions:

1. In a medium bowl, combine tomato, cucumber, and parsley.
2. Drizzle with olive oil and lemon juice.
3. Season with salt and pepper.
4. Toss gently and serve fresh.

Nutritional value per serving: Calories: 90, Carbs: 8g, Fiber: 2g, Sugars: 4g, Protein: 1g, Saturated fat: 0g, Unsaturated fat: 6g

Difficulty rating: ★☆☆☆☆

Tips for ingredient variations: Add a spoonful of cooked chickpeas to make it more filling. Sprinkle with crumbled feta for a Greek-style salad

Desserts – Light, Mediterranean-inspired sweets

Baked Apple with Cinnamon and Raisins

Number of servings: 2

Preparation time: 5 minutes

Cooking time: 25 minutes

Ingredients:

- 2 medium apples (such as Gala or Fuji)
- 2 tbsp raisins
- ½ tsp ground cinnamon
- 1 tsp extra virgin olive oil (optional)
- 2 tsp water

Directions:

1. Preheat oven to 375°F (190°C).
2. Core the apples, leaving the bottom intact to hold the filling.
3. In a small bowl, mix raisins and cinnamon.
4. Stuff the center of each apple with the raisin mixture.
5. Place the apples in a small baking dish. Drizzle lightly with olive oil (if using) and add water to the bottom of the dish.
6. Cover with foil and bake for 20–25 minutes, or until apples are tender.
7. Let cool slightly and serve warm.

Nutritional value per serving: Calories: 140, Carbs: 31g, Fiber: 4g, Sugars: 24g, Protein: 1g, Saturated fat: 0g, Unsaturated fat: 2g

Difficulty rating: ★★☆☆☆

Tips for ingredient variations: Add chopped walnuts for crunch or use chopped dried apricots instead of raisins.

Greek Yogurt with Honey and Crushed Walnuts

Number of servings: 1

Preparation time: 5 minutes

Cooking time: 0 minutes

Ingredients:

- ¾ cup plain Greek yogurt (whole or low-fat)
- 1 tsp honey
- 2 tbsp crushed walnuts

Directions:

1. Place Greek yogurt in a bowl.
2. Drizzle honey evenly over the top.
3. Sprinkle with crushed walnuts.
4. Serve immediately.

Nutritional value per serving: Calories: 260, Carbs: 14g, Fiber: 2g, Sugars: 9g, Protein: 15g, Saturated fat: 2g, Unsaturated fat: 10g

Difficulty rating: ★☆☆☆☆

Tips for ingredient variations: Add a dash of cinnamon or a few fresh berries for extra flavor and color.

Fresh Figs with Ricotta Cheese

Number of servings: 2

Preparation time: 5 minutes
Cooking time: 0 minutes

Ingredients:

- 4 fresh figs, halved
- ½ cup ricotta cheese
- 1 tsp honey (optional)
- Pinch of ground cinnamon (optional)

Directions:

1. Arrange fig halves on a small serving plate.
2. Spoon a small amount of ricotta cheese on top of each fig half.
3. Drizzle lightly with honey, if using.
4. Sprinkle with cinnamon, if desired, and serve immediately.

Nutritional value per serving: Calories: 170, Carbs: 18g, Fiber: 3g, Sugars: 14g, Protein: 6g, Saturated fat: 3g, Unsaturated fat: 2g

Difficulty rating: ★☆☆☆☆

Tips for ingredient variations: Use plain Greek yogurt instead of ricotta for a lighter option. Substitute fresh figs with halved dates if figs are out of season.

Sliced Oranges with Cinnamon

Number of servings: 2
Preparation time: 5 minutes
Cooking time: 0 minutes

Ingredients:

- 2 medium oranges
- ¼ tsp ground cinnamon

Directions:

1. Peel the oranges and slice them into thin rounds.
2. Arrange the slices on a plate, slightly overlapping.
3. Sprinkle lightly with ground cinnamon.
4. Serve immediately or chill for 10 minutes before serving.

Nutritional value per serving: Calories: 80, Carbs: 20g, Fiber: 3g, Sugars: 17g, Protein: 1g, Saturated fat: 0g, Unsaturated fat: 0g

Difficulty rating: ★☆☆☆☆

Tips for ingredient variations: Add a few crushed pistachios or mint leaves for a Mediterranean twist.

Poached Pears with a Dash of Vanilla

Number of servings: 2
Preparation time: 5 minutes
Cooking time: 20 minutes

Ingredients:

- 2 ripe but firm pears, peeled and halved
- 2 cups water
- ½ tsp pure vanilla extract
- ½ tsp ground cinnamon (optional)

Directions:

1. In a small saucepan, bring water and vanilla (and cinnamon, if using) to a simmer.
2. Add the pear halves, cut side down.
3. Cover and simmer gently for 15–20 minutes, until pears are tender but not falling apart.
4. Remove from heat and let cool slightly in the liquid.
5. Serve warm or chilled, with a spoonful of the poaching liquid.

Nutritional value per serving: Calories: 110, Carbs: 26g, Fiber: 4g, Sugars: 17g, Protein: 1g, Fat: 0g

Difficulty rating: ★★☆☆☆

Tips for ingredient variations: Add a strip of lemon or orange peel to the water for extra flavor.

Almond-Date Energy Balls (No Sugar)

Number of servings: 10 (1 ball per serving)

Preparation time: 10 minutes

Cooking time: 0 minutes

Ingredients:

- 1 cup pitted Medjool dates
- ½ cup raw almonds
- 2 tbsp rolled oats
- 1 tbsp chia seeds
- ½ tsp cinnamon
- 1 tbsp water (if needed)

Directions:

1. Add dates, almonds, oats, chia seeds, and cinnamon to a food processor.
2. Pulse until the mixture is crumbly and sticks together when pressed.
3. If too dry, add a tablespoon of water and pulse again.
4. Roll into 10 small balls using your hands.
5. Store in the fridge for up to 1 week.

Nutritional value per serving: Calories: 100, Carbs: 13g, Fiber: 2g, Sugars: 9g, Protein: 2g, Unsaturated fat: 4g

Difficulty rating: ★☆☆☆☆

Tips for ingredient variations: Swap almonds with walnuts or add shredded coconut for texture.

Fresh Peach Slices with Mint and Plain Yogurt

Number of servings: 1

Preparation time: 5 minutes

Cooking time: 0 minutes

Ingredients:

- 1 ripe peach, sliced
- ½ cup plain Greek yogurt
- 1 tsp chopped fresh mint

Directions:

1. Place peach slices in a small bowl or dessert dish.
2. Top with a generous dollop of yogurt.
3. Sprinkle with chopped mint.
4. Serve immediately.

Nutritional value per serving: Calories: 120, Carbs: 15g, Fiber: 2g, Sugars: 12g, Protein: 7g, Fat: 4g

Difficulty rating: ★☆☆☆☆

Tips for ingredient variations: Use nectarines or plums if peaches are out of season. Add a dash of cinnamon if desired.

Chia Pudding Made with Almond Milk and Fruit

Number of servings: 2

Preparation time: 5 minutes (plus 4+ hours chill time)

Cooking time: 0 minutes

Ingredients:

- ¼ cup chia seeds
- 1 cup unsweetened almond milk
- ½ tsp vanilla extract (optional)
- ½ cup fresh or frozen berries

Directions:

1. In a bowl or jar, whisk together chia seeds, almond milk, and vanilla.
2. Cover and refrigerate for at least 4 hours or overnight, until thickened.
3. Stir well before serving and top with berries.
4. Serve chilled.

Nutritional value per serving: Calories: 150, Carbs: 12g, Fiber: 8g, Sugars: 3g, Protein: 4g, Fat: 8g

Difficulty rating: ★☆☆☆☆

Tips for ingredient variations: Use oat milk instead of almond milk. Add sliced banana or a drizzle of honey if extra sweetness is needed.

Roasted Grapes with a Touch of Balsamic

Number of servings: 2

Preparation time: 5 minutes

Cooking time: 15 minutes

Ingredients:

- 1 cup red or black seedless grapes
- 1 tsp extra virgin olive oil
- 1 tsp balsamic vinegar

Directions:

1. Preheat the oven to 375°F (190°C).
2. Place grapes on a small baking sheet lined with parchment paper.
3. Drizzle with olive oil and balsamic vinegar.
4. Gently toss to coat.
5. Roast for 15 minutes, until the grapes are soft and slightly caramelized.
6. Let cool slightly before serving. Can be enjoyed warm or at room temperature.

Nutritional value per serving: Calories: 90, Carbs: 17g, Fiber: 1g, Sugars: 14g, Protein: 0g, Saturated fat: 0g, Unsaturated fat: 3g

Difficulty rating: ★☆☆☆☆

Tips for ingredient variations: Use a mix of red and green grapes for more color. Serve over plain yogurt for extra protein.

Blended Frozen Banana ("Nice Cream")

Number of servings: 2

Preparation time: 5 minutes (plus freeze time)

Cooking time: 0 minutes

Ingredients:

- 2 ripe bananas, sliced and frozen
- 1–2 tbsp unsweetened almond milk (optional, for blending)

Directions:

1. Peel and slice ripe bananas. Freeze them for at least 4 hours or overnight.
2. Place frozen banana slices in a food processor or high-powered blender.
3. Blend until smooth and creamy, adding almond milk if needed to help blend.
4. For a firmer texture, freeze for 30 minutes or serve right away as soft-serve..

Nutritional value per serving: Calories: 105, Carbs: 27g, Fiber: 3g, Sugars: 14g, Protein: 1g, Saturated fat: 0g, Unsaturated fat: 0g

Difficulty rating: ★☆☆☆☆

Tips for ingredient variations: Add a dash of cinnamon or blend with a few frozen berries. Top with chopped walnuts for a crunch.

Baked Plums with a Drizzle of Olive Oil

Number of servings: 2

Preparation time: 5 minutes

Cooking time: 20 minutes

Ingredients:

- 2 ripe plums, halved and pitted
- 1 tsp extra virgin olive oil
- Pinch of cinnamon (optional)

Directions:

1. Preheat oven to 375°F (190°C).
2. Place plum halves cut-side up in a small baking dish.
3. Drizzle with olive oil and sprinkle with cinnamon if using.
4. Bake for 20 minutes, until soft and bubbling.
5. Let cool slightly before serving.

Nutritional value per serving: Calories: 80, Carbs: 18g, Fiber: 2g, Sugars: 15g, Protein: 0g, Saturated fat: 0g, Unsaturated fat: 4g

Difficulty rating: ★☆☆☆☆

Tips for ingredient variations: Add a dollop of plain Greek yogurt on top. Try with peaches or nectarines in season.

Square of Dark Chocolate with Berries

Number of servings: 1

Preparation time: 2 minutes

Cooking time: 0 minutes

Ingredients:

- 1 square (about 1 oz) dark chocolate (70% cocoa or higher)
- ¼ cup fresh berries (blueberries, raspberries, or strawberries)

Directions:

1. Place the chocolate square on a small plate.
2. Add fresh berries on the side or on top.
3. Enjoy slowly, savoring each bite.

Nutritional value per serving: Calories: 140, Carbs: 12g, Fiber: 3g, Sugars: 7g, Protein: 2g, Saturated fat: 4g, Unsaturated fat: 5g

Difficulty rating: ★☆☆☆☆

Tips for ingredient variations: Try pairing with sliced oranges or apple slices. Make sure to choose unsweetened, high-quality dark chocolate.

Ricotta with Unsweetened Cocoa and Honey

Number of servings: 1

Preparation time: 5 minutes

Cooking time: 0 minutes

Ingredients:

- ½ cup whole milk ricotta
- 1 tsp unsweetened cocoa powder
- 1 tsp honey
- Pinch of cinnamon (optional)

Directions:

1. Place ricotta in a small bowl.
2. Sprinkle with cocoa powder and stir gently until well combined.
3. Drizzle with honey and a pinch of cinnamon, if using.
4. Serve immediately or chill briefly before eating.

Nutritional value per serving: Calories: 180, Carbs: 9g, Fiber: 1g, Sugars: 6g, Protein: 9g, Saturated fat: 4g, Unsaturated fat: 3g

Difficulty rating: ★☆☆☆☆

Tips for ingredient variations: Add a few crushed walnuts or sliced strawberries for extra texture and flavor.

Oat-Almond Cookies (No Refined Sugar)

Number of servings: 12 cookies

Preparation time: 10 minutes

Cooking time: 15 minutes

Ingredients:

- 1 cup rolled oats
- ½ cup almond flour
- 1 ripe banana, mashed
- ¼ cup almond butter
- ¼ cup chopped almonds
- ¼ cup raisins or chopped dates
- 1 tsp cinnamon
- 1 tsp vanilla extract

Directions:

1. Preheat oven to 350°F (175°C) and line a baking sheet with parchment paper.
2. In a bowl, mix mashed banana, almond butter, and vanilla until smooth.
3. Add oats, almond flour, cinnamon, raisins (or dates), and chopped almonds. Mix until combined.
4. Scoop tablespoon-sized portions onto the baking sheet and flatten gently.
5. Bake for 12–15 minutes, until lightly golden.
6. Let cool before serving.

Nutritional value per cookie: Calories: 120, Carbs: 13g, Fiber: 2g, Sugars: 4g, Protein: 3g, Saturated fat: 0.5g, Unsaturated fat: 6g

Difficulty rating: ★★☆☆☆

Tips for ingredient variations: Use chopped dried apricots instead of raisins. Add a pinch of sea salt for contrast.

Fresh Fruit Salad with Lemon Zest and Mint

Number of servings: 2

Preparation time: 10 minutes

Cooking time: 0 minutes

Ingredients:

- ½ cup strawberries, sliced
- ½ cup orange segments
- ½ cup diced apple
- ½ banana, sliced
- 1 tsp lemon zest
- 1 tsp lemon juice
- 4 fresh mint leaves, chopped

Directions:

1. Combine all fruits in a mixing bowl.
2. Add lemon zest, lemon juice, and chopped mint.
3. Gently toss until the fruit is well coated.
4. Serve immediately or refrigerate for 15–20 minutes before serving.

Nutritional value per serving: Calories: 100, Carbs: 24g, Fiber: 3g, Sugars: 16g, Protein: 1g, Saturated fat: 0g, Unsaturated fat: 0g

Difficulty rating: ★☆☆☆☆

Tips for ingredient variations: Use seasonal fruits like kiwi, grapes, or melon. Add a sprinkle of chia seeds for fiber.

60 Day Meal Plan

Day 1

- **Breakfast:** Greek yogurt with honey, walnuts & blueberries
- **Lunch:** Lentil and vegetable stew
- **Side:** Roasted carrots with olive oil and thyme
- **Dinner:** Baked salmon with olive oil and herbs
- **Dessert:** Baked apple with cinnamon and raisins

Day 2

- **Breakfast:** Rolled oats with chia seeds, raisins & cinnamon
- **Lunch:** Chickpea and spinach sauté with garlic
- **Side:** Cucumber yogurt salad with mint
- **Dinner:** Lemon and rosemary baked chicken thighs
- **Dessert:** Greek yogurt with honey and crushed walnuts

Day 3

- **Breakfast:** Whole grain toast with mashed avocado and olive oil
- **Lunch:** Grilled eggplant with tomato and crumbled feta
- **Side:** Steamed broccoli with lemon drizzle
- **Dinner:** Cod in tomato-olive sauce
- **Dessert:** Fresh figs with ricotta cheese

Day 4

- **Breakfast:** Scrambled eggs with spinach and cherry tomatoes
- **Lunch:** Stuffed bell peppers with brown rice, herbs, and olives
- **Side:** Tomato and red onion salad
- **Dinner:** Chicken and lentil one-pan meal
- **Dessert:** Sliced oranges with cinnamon

Day 5

- **Breakfast:** Cottage cheese with sliced peaches and slivered almonds
- **Lunch:** Farro salad with cucumber, tomato, and parsley
- **Side:** Roasted zucchini with oregano
- **Dinner:** Mediterranean fish stew with tomatoes and potatoes
- **Dessert:** Poached pears with a dash of vanilla

Day 6

- **Breakfast:** Boiled eggs with whole grain crackers and cucumber
- **Lunch:** Cauliflower and chickpea skillet
- **Side:** Beet and orange salad
- **Dinner:** Baked chicken breast with capers and parsley
- **Dessert:** Almond-date energy balls (no sugar)

Day 7

- **Breakfast:** Banana with peanut butter and ground flaxseed
- **Lunch:** White bean and rosemary soup
- **Side:** Lentil salad with lemon dressing
- **Dinner:** Tuna and white bean salad with parsley
- **Dessert:** Fresh peach slices with mint and plain yogurt

Day 8

- **Breakfast:** Plain yogurt with apple slices and sunflower seeds
- **Lunch:** Vegetable tagine with chickpeas and almonds
- **Side:** Cabbage salad with olive oil and vinegar
- **Dinner:** Grilled trout with garlic and lemon
- **Dessert:** Chia pudding made with almond milk and fruit

Day 9

- **Breakfast:** Mediterranean herb omelet with olive oil
- **Lunch:** Quinoa bowl with roasted vegetables and lemon dressing
- **Side:** Grilled eggplant rounds with olive oil
- **Dinner:** Stewed chicken with chickpeas and tomato
- **Dessert:** Roasted grapes with a touch of balsamic

Day 10

- **Breakfast:** Overnight oats with almond milk and frozen berries
- **Lunch:** Zucchini and tomato bake with oregano and olive oil
- **Side:** Olive tapenade with whole grain crackers
- **Dinner:** Broiled mackerel with lemon
- **Dessert:** Blended frozen banana ("nice cream")

Day 11

- **Breakfast:** Whole wheat toast with tahini and a drizzle of honey
- **Lunch:** Tomato and white bean skillet

- **Side:** Quinoa with parsley and olive oil
- **Dinner:** Grilled chicken breast with Mediterranean herb rub
- **Dessert:** Baked plums with a drizzle of olive oil

Day 12

- **Breakfast:** Smoothie with spinach, banana, and plain yogurt
- **Lunch:** Baked sweet potato topped with hummus and greens
- **Side:** Blanched green beans with slivered almonds
- **Dinner:** Shrimp sautéed with garlic and greens
- **Dessert:** Square of dark chocolate with berries

Day 13

- **Breakfast:** Hard-boiled eggs with orange slices and whole grain toast
- **Lunch:** Whole grain pasta with sautéed greens and garlic
- **Side:** Roasted sweet potato wedges
- **Dinner:** Foil-baked cod with zucchini and lemon
- **Dessert:** Ricotta with unsweetened cocoa and honey

Day 14

- **Breakfast:** Ricotta on toast with sliced fresh figs
- **Lunch:** Greek-style baked butter beans (Gigantes Plaki)
- **Side:** Tomato, cucumber, and parsley bowl
- **Dinner:** Chicken with garlic sautéed spinach
- **Dessert:** Oat-almond cookies (no refined sugar)

Day 15

- **Breakfast:** Warm barley porridge with chopped nuts and dates
- **Lunch:** Mushroom and brown rice risotto
- **Side:** Marinated mushrooms with herbs
- **Dinner:** Cold salmon salad with cucumber and yogurt dressing
- **Dessert:** Fresh fruit salad with lemon zest and mint

Day 16

- **Breakfast:** Pita with hummus and cucumber rounds
- **Lunch:** Pasta e fagioli (pasta and beans, no meat broth)
- **Side:** Sautéed greens with lemon
- **Dinner:** Baked haddock with capers and olive oil
- **Dessert:** Greek yogurt with honey and crushed walnuts

Day 17

- **Breakfast:** Whole grain cereal with milk and sliced strawberries
- **Lunch:** Lentil and eggplant moussaka (no red meat)
- **Side:** Cucumber yogurt salad with mint
- **Dinner:** Grilled swordfish with lemon and herbs
- **Dessert:** Sliced oranges with cinnamon

Day 18

- **Breakfast:** Egg muffins with vegetables and herbs
- **Lunch:** Falafel baked in the oven with tahini
- **Side:** Couscous with lemon and mint
- **Dinner:** Tuna, chickpea, and arugula bowl
- **Dessert:** Almond-date energy balls (no sugar)

Day 19

- **Breakfast:** Quinoa breakfast bowl with yogurt and fruit
- **Lunch:** Chickpea and vegetable stuffed eggplant
- **Side:** Simple Greek salad with feta and olives
- **Dinner:** Anchovy and tomato whole grain flatbread
- **Dessert:** Fresh peach slices with mint and plain yogurt

Day 20

- **Breakfast:** Roasted sweet potato slices with tahini and chopped pistachios
- **Lunch:** Grilled vegetable skewers with halloumi
- **Side:** Roasted peppers with garlic and olive oil
- **Dinner:** Poached salmon with dill and lemon
- **Dessert:** Poached pears with a dash of vanilla

Day 21

- **Breakfast:** Greek yogurt with honey, walnuts & blueberries
- **Lunch:** Vegetable lasagna with whole grain pasta and ricotta
- **Side:** Lentil salad with lemon dressing
- **Dinner:** Halibut baked with cherry tomatoes and onions
- **Dessert:** Chia pudding made with almond milk and fruit

Day 22

- **Breakfast:** Rolled oats with chia seeds, raisins & cinnamon
- **Lunch:** Cauliflower steaks with yogurt and za'atar
- **Side:** Beet and orange salad
- **Dinner:** Chicken skillet with farro and greens
- **Dessert:** Baked apple with cinnamon and raisins

Day 23

- **Breakfast:** Whole grain toast with mashed avocado and olive oil
- **Lunch:** White bean and rosemary soup
- **Side:** Roasted carrots with olive oil and thyme
- **Dinner:** Mussels in a light tomato broth with herbs
- **Dessert:** Ricotta with unsweetened cocoa and honey

Day 24

- **Breakfast:** Scrambled eggs with spinach and cherry tomatoes
- **Lunch:** Stuffed bell peppers with brown rice, herbs, and olives
- **Side:** Roasted zucchini with oregano
- **Dinner:** Chicken roll-ups with feta, spinach, and herbs
- **Dessert:** Fresh fruit salad with lemon zest and mint

Day 25

- **Breakfast:** Cottage cheese with sliced peaches and slivered almonds
- **Lunch:** Baked tofu with lemon, garlic, and olive oil
- **Side:** Couscous with lemon and mint
- **Dinner:** Tuna and quinoa cakes
- **Dessert:** Square of dark chocolate with berries

Day 26

- **Breakfast:** Boiled eggs with whole grain crackers and cucumber
- **Lunch:** Greek-style baked butter beans (Gigantes Plaki)
- **Side:** Tomato, cucumber, and parsley bowl
- **Dinner:** Lemon and rosemary baked chicken thighs
- **Dessert:** Roasted grapes with a touch of balsamic

Day 27

- **Breakfast:** Banana with peanut butter and ground flaxseed
- **Lunch:** Quinoa bowl with roasted vegetables and lemon dressing
- **Side:** Grilled eggplant rounds with olive oil
- **Dinner:** Foil-baked cod with zucchini and lemon
- **Dessert:** Baked plums with a drizzle of olive oil

Day 28

- **Breakfast:** Plain yogurt with apple slices and sunflower seeds
- **Lunch:** Lentil and vegetable stew
- **Side:** Olive tapenade with whole grain crackers
- **Dinner:** Grilled trout with garlic and lemon
- **Dessert:** Almond-date energy balls (no sugar)

Day 29

- **Breakfast:** Mediterranean herb omelet with olive oil
- **Lunch:** Pasta e fagioli (pasta and beans, no meat broth)
- **Side:** Blanched green beans with slivered almonds
- **Dinner:** Salmon patties with yogurt dill sauce
- **Dessert:** Poached pears with a dash of vanilla

Day 30

- **Breakfast:** Overnight oats with almond milk and frozen berries
- **Lunch:** Chickpea and spinach sauté with garlic
- **Side:** Cabbage salad with olive oil and vinegar
- **Dinner:** Grilled swordfish with lemon and herbs
- **Dessert:** Greek yogurt with honey and crushed walnuts

Day 31

- **Breakfast:** Whole wheat toast with tahini and a drizzle of honey
- **Lunch:** Farro salad with cucumber, tomato, and parsley
- **Side:** Steamed broccoli with lemon drizzle
- **Dinner:** Baked chicken breast with capers and parsley
- **Dessert:** Blended frozen banana ("nice cream")

Day 32

- **Breakfast:** Smoothie with spinach, banana, and plain yogurt
- **Lunch:** Tomato and white bean skillet

- **Side:** Marinated mushrooms with herbs
- **Dinner:** Poached salmon with dill and lemon
- **Dessert:** Sliced oranges with cinnamon

Day 33

- **Breakfast:** Hard-boiled eggs with orange slices and whole grain toast
- **Lunch:** Gnocchi with cherry tomatoes and basil
- **Side:** Quinoa with parsley and olive oil
- **Dinner:** Chicken with garlic sautéed spinach
- **Dessert:** Fresh peach slices with mint and plain yogurt

Day 34

- **Breakfast:** Ricotta on toast with sliced fresh figs
- **Lunch:** Cauliflower and chickpea skillet
- **Side:** Tomato and red onion salad
- **Dinner:** Broiled mackerel with lemon
- **Dessert:** Chia pudding made with almond milk and fruit

Day 35

- **Breakfast:** Warm barley porridge with chopped nuts and dates
- **Lunch:** Chickpea and vegetable stuffed eggplant
- **Side:** Sautéed greens with lemon
- **Dinner:** Tuna and white bean salad with parsley
- **Dessert:** Oat-almond cookies (no refined sugar)

Day 36

- **Breakfast:** Pita with hummus and cucumber rounds
- **Lunch:** Vegetable tagine with chickpeas and almonds
- **Side:** Roasted sweet potato wedges
- **Dinner:** Grilled chicken breast with Mediterranean herb rub
- **Dessert:** Greek yogurt with honey and crushed walnuts

Day 37

- **Breakfast:** Whole grain cereal with milk and sliced strawberries
- **Lunch:** Mushroom and brown rice risotto
- **Side:** Beet and orange salad
- **Dinner:** Cod in tomato-olive sauce
- **Dessert:** Baked apple with cinnamon and raisins

Day 38

- **Breakfast:** Egg muffins with vegetables and herbs
- **Lunch:** Falafel baked in the oven with tahini
- **Side:** Roasted carrots with olive oil and thyme
- **Dinner:** Cold salmon salad with cucumber and yogurt dressing
- **Dessert:** Poached pears with a dash of vanilla

Day 39

- **Breakfast:** Quinoa breakfast bowl with yogurt and fruit
- **Lunch:** Grilled vegetable skewers with halloumi
- **Side:** Tomato, cucumber, and parsley bowl
- **Dinner:** Baked haddock with capers and olive oil
- **Dessert:** Ricotta with unsweetened cocoa and honey

Day 40

- **Breakfast:** Roasted sweet potato slices with tahini and chopped pistachios
- **Lunch:** Lentil and eggplant moussaka (no red meat)
- **Side:** Cucumber yogurt salad with mint
- **Dinner:** Shrimp sautéed with garlic and greens
- **Dessert:** Roasted grapes with a touch of balsamic

Day 41

- **Breakfast:** Greek yogurt with honey, walnuts & blueberries
- **Lunch:** Lentil and vegetable stew
- **Side:** Cabbage salad with olive oil and vinegar
- **Dinner:** Tuna, chickpea, and arugula bowl
- **Dessert:** Fresh fruit salad with lemon zest and mint

Day 42

- **Breakfast:** Rolled oats with chia seeds, raisins & cinnamon
- **Lunch:** Vegetable lasagna with whole grain pasta and ricotta
- **Side:** Steamed broccoli with lemon drizzle
- **Dinner:** Chicken and lentil one-pan meal
- **Dessert:** Chia pudding made with almond milk and fruit

Day 43

- **Breakfast:** Whole grain toast with mashed avocado and olive oil

- **Lunch:** Baked tofu with lemon, garlic, and olive oil
- **Side:** Roasted peppers with garlic and olive oil
- **Dinner:** Mediterranean fish stew with tomatoes and potatoes
- **Dessert:** Sliced oranges with cinnamon

Day 44

- **Breakfast:** Scrambled eggs with spinach and cherry tomatoes
- **Lunch:** Tomato and white bean skillet
- **Side:** Couscous with lemon and mint
- **Dinner:** Grilled swordfish with lemon and herbs
- **Dessert:** Square of dark chocolate with berries

Day 45

- **Breakfast:** Cottage cheese with sliced peaches and slivered almonds
- **Lunch:** Quinoa bowl with roasted vegetables and lemon dressing
- **Side:** Lentil salad with lemon dressing
- **Dinner:** Poached salmon with dill and lemon
- **Dessert:** Baked apple with cinnamon and raisins

Day 46

- **Breakfast:** Boiled eggs with whole grain crackers and cucumber
- **Lunch:** Whole grain pasta with sautéed greens and garlic
- **Side:** Beet and orange salad
- **Dinner:** Lemon and rosemary baked chicken thighs
- **Dessert:** Almond-date energy balls (no sugar)

Day 47

- **Breakfast:** Banana with peanut butter and ground flaxseed
- **Lunch:** White bean and rosemary soup
- **Side:** Blanched green beans with slivered almonds
- **Dinner:** Baked salmon with olive oil and herbs
- **Dessert:** Fresh peach slices with mint and plain yogurt

Day 48

- **Breakfast:** Plain yogurt with apple slices and sunflower seeds
- **Lunch:** Stuffed bell peppers with brown rice, herbs, and olives
- **Side:** Tomato and red onion salad
- **Dinner:** Broiled mackerel with lemon
- **Dessert:** Ricotta with unsweetened cocoa and honey

Day 49

- **Breakfast:** Mediterranean herb omelet with olive oil
- **Lunch:** Chickpea and spinach sauté with garlic
- **Side:** Marinated mushrooms with herbs
- **Dinner:** Baked haddock with capers and olive oil
- **Dessert:** Baked plums with a drizzle of olive oil

Day 50

- **Breakfast:** Overnight oats with almond milk and frozen berries
- **Lunch:** Pasta e fagioli (pasta and beans, no meat broth)
- **Side:** Grilled eggplant rounds with olive oil
- **Dinner:** Chicken roll-ups with feta, spinach, and herbs
- **Dessert:** Blended frozen banana ("nice cream")

Day 51

- **Breakfast:** Whole wheat toast with tahini and a drizzle of honey
- **Lunch:** Mushroom and brown rice risotto
- **Side:** Olive tapenade with whole grain crackers
- **Dinner:** Foil-baked cod with zucchini and lemon
- **Dessert:** Greek yogurt with honey and crushed walnuts

Day 52

- **Breakfast:** Smoothie with spinach, banana, and plain yogurt
- **Lunch:** Greek-style baked butter beans (Gigantes Plaki)
- **Side:** Couscous with lemon and mint
- **Dinner:** Tuna-stuffed tomatoes with capers
- **Dessert:** Poached pears with a dash of vanilla

Day 53

- **Breakfast:** Hard-boiled eggs with orange slices and whole grain toast
- **Lunch:** Vegetable tagine with chickpeas and almonds
- **Side:** Roasted sweet potato wedges
- **Dinner:** Chicken with garlic sautéed spinach
- **Dessert:** Chia pudding made with almond milk and fruit

Day 54

- **Breakfast:** Ricotta on toast with sliced fresh figs
- **Lunch:** Falafel baked in the oven with tahini
- **Side:** Tomato, cucumber, and parsley bowl
- **Dinner:** Shrimp sautéed with garlic and greens
- **Dessert:** Fresh fruit salad with lemon zest and mint

Day 55

- **Breakfast:** Warm barley porridge with chopped nuts and dates
- **Lunch:** Zucchini fritters with yogurt sauce
- **Side:** Cabbage salad with olive oil and vinegar
- **Dinner:** Grilled chicken breast with Mediterranean herb rub
- **Dessert:** Almond-date energy balls (no sugar)

Day 56

- **Breakfast:** Pita with hummus and cucumber rounds
- **Lunch:** Gnocchi with cherry tomatoes and basil
- **Side:** Roasted carrots with olive oil and thyme
- **Dinner:** Cold salmon salad with cucumber and yogurt dressing
- **Dessert:** Poached pears with a dash of vanilla

Day 57

- **Breakfast:** Whole grain cereal with milk and sliced strawberries
- **Lunch:** Chickpea and vegetable stuffed eggplant
- **Side:** Sautéed greens with lemon
- **Dinner:** Cod in tomato-olive sauce
- **Dessert:** Oat-almond cookies (no refined sugar)

Day 58

- **Breakfast:** Egg muffins with vegetables and herbs
- **Lunch:** Grilled vegetable skewers with halloumi
- **Side:** Tomato and red onion salad
- **Dinner:** Tuna and white bean salad with parsley
- **Dessert:** Ricotta with unsweetened cocoa and honey

Day 59

- **Breakfast:** Quinoa breakfast bowl with yogurt and fruit
- **Lunch:** Lentil and eggplant moussaka (no red meat)
- **Side:** Blanched green beans with slivered almonds
- **Dinner:** Chicken and lentil one-pan meal
- **Dessert:** Roasted grapes with a touch of balsamic

Day 60

- **Breakfast:** Roasted sweet potato slices with tahini and chopped pistachios
- **Lunch:** Grilled eggplant with tomato and crumbled feta
- **Side:** Couscous with lemon and mint
- **Dinner:** Poached salmon with dill and lemon
- **Dessert:** Fresh peach slices with mint and plain yogurt

Final Words: Keep It Simple, Keep It Real

You don't have to change everything about your current diet to feel better, nor do you need to follow a strict set of rules. You're learning to make healthier choices and cook food in a way you truly enjoy. Your food choices should suit your body and daily routine.

Because it's a lifestyle, not a fad, it's much easier to ease into. As you do, you'll learn how to incorporate healthier, fresher foods, and you'll start to notice the changes in your energy levels, reduction in pain, improvements in mobility, and have a better quality of life. The benefits make it much easier to keep following the diet.

You have already made a lot of progress since you've reached this point. It means you are interested in learning more and looking for ways to improve your life. You obviously want a plan that is practical and sustainable. And that's the right mindset to succeed with this diet.

Here are the key takeaways as you prepare to make the change:

1. Keep meals simple.
2. Eat foods that make you feel good—not just in the moment, but hours later.
3. Move your body, even a little.
4. Eat with others when you can, or at least eat without rushing.
5. Listen to your needs because they matter.

When's the best time to start making these changes? Whenever you are ready. Start small, making just one or two adjustments at a time. Then you can start to build from those small beginnings.

WAIT—THERE'S MORE TO ENJOY!

Congratulations on taking a wonderful step toward feeling better, living longer, and enjoying every bite along the way!

To make your Mediterranean lifestyle even simpler and more satisfying, I've prepared something extra—just for you.

GET 30 FREE BONUS RECIPES—EXCLUSIVELY FOR READERS!

Healthy eating should always be easy, joyful, and full of flavor.

These additional Mediterranean-inspired recipes were created to add even more variety and taste to your daily routine—helping you stay on track without ever feeling restricted.

Just scan the QR code to instantly download your FREE BONUS RECIPES.

Because taking care of yourself should feel rewarding every step of the way—and taste absolutely delicious!

Made in the USA
Coppell, TX
09 August 2025

52754871R00046